D-DAY

THE ALLIED INVASION OF NORMANDY

For Private Harry 'Butch' Firman,
BREN GUNNER

Ox & Bucks Light Infantry

King's Own Scottish Borderers

Duke of Cornwall's Light Infantry

Written By Mike Lepine

Danann
BOOKS

'They fight not for the lust of conquest. They fight to end conquest. They fight to liberate.'
PRESIDENT FRANKLIN D. ROOSEVELT, RADIO MESSAGE TO THE NATION 6 JUNE, 1944

'This vast operation is undoubtedly the most complicated and difficult that has ever occurred.'
WINSTON CHURCHILL, ADDRESSING THE HOUSE OF COMMONS, 6 JUNE, 1944

'We want to get the hell over there. The quicker we clean up this goddamned mess, the quicker we can take a little jaunt against the purple pissing Japs and clean out their nest too. Before the goddamned Marines get all of the credit.'
GENERAL GEORGE PATTON

'This operation is not being planned with any alternatives. This operation is planned as a victory, and that's the way it's going to be. We're going down there, and we're throwing everything we have into it, and we're going to make it a success.'
GENERAL DWIGHT EISENHOWER

'When I think of the beaches of Normandy choked with the flower of American and British youth, and when, in my mind's eye, I see the tides running red with their blood, I have my doubts…I have my doubts.'
WINSTON CHURCHILL

'The best part of the invasion is that I have the feeling that friends are approaching…'
ANNE FRANK

BOOKS

© Danann Publishing Limited 2019

First Published Danann Publishing Ltd 2019

WARNING: For private domestic use only, any unauthorised Copying, hiring,
lending or public performance of this book is illegal.

CAT NO: DAN0418

Photography courtesy of

Getty images:

Arterra/UIG	Keystone / Stringer	Corbis
Popperfoto	IWM	LAPI/Roger Viollet
Bettmann	Smith Collection/Gado	Andia/UIG

Other images Wiki Commons

Book layout & design Darren Grice at Ctrl-d

Copy editor Tom O'Neill

Made in EU.

ISBN: 978-1-912332-30-4

CONTENTS

DIEPPE OPERATION JUBILEE

At 0450 hours on 19 August 1942, 5,000 Canadian troops and 1,000 British soldiers — along with fifty-eight Churchill tanks — stormed the stony beaches of Dieppe, a fishing port in the Normandy region of France. The plan was to seize the port, hold it for at least two tides and then withdraw gracefully.

The German defenders knew they were coming – and they were ready and waiting.

The main assault was met by murderous fire from well positioned machine gun nests and pill boxes. Fields of barbed wire held the soldiers on the beach while they were hammered by the guns. Some units did make it off the beach, but they suffered further heavy casualties in the town, and those who reached open countryside were quickly forced back to the port by newly-arrived German reinforcements.

The contingent of Churchill tanks proved useless. Only twenty-nine of the fifty-eight were successfully landed. Twelve got hopelessly bogged down at the sea's edge and fought from there until they were picked off and destroyed. Fifteen made it up and over the sea wall but almost immediately got jammed up by concrete anti-tank obstacles and could not follow the troops into the town. Instead, they were forced to retreat onto the beach again and provide what covering fire they could from there until their crews were either killed or taken prisoner.

Above the port, the RAF and RCAF were locked together with the Luftwaffe in one of the largest air battles ever fought, with 74 Allied squadrons committed to supporting the raid and providing a shield against Luftwaffe attacks on the landing beaches.

By 1100, it was obvious that the attack had been a failure, and the scramble began to rescue as many troops as possible. The evacuation ended by 1400. The Canadian forces had lost 3,367 men killed, wounded or taken prisoner. British Commandos suffered 275 casualties. A Royal Navy destroyer had been lost in the action along with thirty-three landing craft. The RAF and RCAF lost 106 Aircraft compared with Luftwaffe losses of just forty-eight planes.

LEARNING LESSONS

'I have no doubt that the Battle of Normandy was won on the beaches of Dieppe. For every man who died in Dieppe, at least 10 more must have been spared in Normandy in 1944.'

Vice-Admiral Lord Louis Mountbatten

Dieppe was a disaster by any measure – but the Allies at least could learn some hard lessons.

It had proved impossible to capture a well defended port with a front-on assault. This was the main conclusion after Dieppe — and it shook the Allies. When the time came for the invasion of Europe, they would be certain to need port facilities right from the very start to keep the invasion force supplied.

The element of surprise was key. The Germans had learned about Dieppe from traitors amongst the French resistance. When the invasion finally came, the Germans needed to be caught off-guard. Secrecy was essential. Total misdirection would be even better.

Conventional armour had failed on the beaches. There had to be a better way of getting armour ashore to support the assault troops — and helping them to overcome anti-tank obstacles.

Beach obstacles were also a serious threat to incoming landing craft and troops moving up the beach, along with barbed wire and minefields. These obstacles needed to be dealt with effectively to ensure a successful beach assault.

Air superiority was vital, both during the invasion and in the days, weeks and months to follow.

MAIN IMAGE: Armoured vehicles used in the raid on Dieppe return to Britain

---

EARLY PLANS

These hard lessons were not lost on the men planning for D-Day.

Nazi Germany had declared war on the United States of America four days after the Japanese attack on Pearl Harbor on 7 December 1941. By the time British Prime Minister Winston Churchill came to America at the end of December, President Franklin D. Roosevelt and his Chiefs of Staff had already decided on the policy of '*Germany First*'. The defeat of Imperial Japan could wait. It had not been an easy decision to reach. A number of American commanders then regarded Britain and its Empire, if not as an enemy, then as a great rival in the battle for world trade. Those of Irish descent hated the British for historical reasons. Those of German or Italian descent were unenthusiastic about targeting their own roots. Roosevelt however, was wise enough to make his plans based on strategic common sense. Germany it would be.

It was evident from the very first days that defeating Nazi Germany would involve an invasion of Europe. At the Arcadia conference on 31 December 1941, America committed to Bolero — a massive build-up of forces in Britain. With the first American officers and 4,000 troops shipped into Britain in January 1942 came a very real impatience to close with the enemy. American commanders started dreaming of an invasion of Europe that very same year. The British were far more cautious. The Americans then suggested Operation Roundup — an invasion in April 1943 with, essentially, whatever was available then. Just pile in and go. The British nodded their heads, careful not to crush American enthusiasms, while secretly consigning the plan to the dustbin of history and gently nudging America in other directions.

The failure of the raid on Dieppe in August 1942 proved sobering, even to the Americans. Talk of an invasion of Europe in 1943 was obviously nonsense. Instead, the British satiated the American lust for action by selling them on Operation Torch, amphibious landings against Vichy French territories in North Africa in November 1942.

At the Casablanca conference in January 1943, the British further delayed landings in France by suggesting Operation Husky — the invasion of Sicily — and then an advance onwards to Italy itself. Churchill had long entertained the idea that Germany could be attacked via the '*soft underbelly*' of Europe — up through Italy, then the Balkans and then Austria and southern Germany. It was something that the Americans, with their far more direct approach, would never agree to, but Churchill kept hoping. The Americans returning home from Casablanca quickly realised that they had allowed the British to commit them to a '*side show*'. Some even suspected that Churchill had got them to commit American boys to fighting for the interests of the British Empire in the Mediterranean. At Casablanca, the Americans had at least forced from the British a commitment to invading France in 1944. The American seized on that and would not let go of it, no matter how much the British talked about the Balkans or further precautionary delays.

At the Trident conference in Washington in May 1943, the Americans forced the British to set the date of the invasion of France for 1 May 1944. This date was confirmed later in August at the Quadrant conference in Quebec. Now, everyone had a target date to work to.

Throughout the winter of 1943-44, the British needled the Americans by sharing with them every single doubt they had. Churchill agonised that '*…this is much the greatest thing we have ever done*' — and he was getting cold feet. Behind the scenes, the British had already decided amongst themselves that the date of 1 May was not set in stone and that Operation Overlord, as it was now becoming known, might somehow be side-lined if opportunities arose for a better action.

Despite all the British hesitation, the Americans insisted on ploughing ahead with Overlord. British Lieutenant- General Frederick Morgan was appointed COSSAC — Chief of Staff to the Supreme Allied Commander — in April 1943. In the absence of a Supreme Allied Commander actually having been appointed, he had responsibility for moving Overlord ahead. And he, it transpired, shared some of Britain's misgivings. On 15 July 1943, he wrote:

'*An Operation of the magnitude of Operation Overlord has never been previously attempted in history. It is fraught with hazards, both in nature and magnitude…Unless these hazards are squarely faced and adequately overcome, the operation cannot succeed.*'

Morgan and his men were charged with identifying potential invasion beaches. To qualify they had to be close enough for effective air cover from England, not too far from the south or south west coast to allow a reasonably timed crossing, they could not come hard up against cliffs and German defences could not be strong. The Pas de Calais was almost immediately ruled out because the Germans had concentrated their forces there. Brittany was ruled out as too far away. This just left the Cotentin Peninsula and Normandy. By Spring 1943, Normandy it was.

HOBART'S FUNNIES

The defeat at Dieppe exposed not only the problems with storming a heavily-guarded port but with attacking anywhere that had solid fortifications and obstacles. It revealed too the practical problems of landing support armour in any meaningful numbers.

Britain already had some experience in developing and using armour that had been modified to perform special tasks. These included Matilda tanks that had been fitted with huge threshing chains to detonate minefields in the Western Desert. In 1943, General Sir Alan Brooke, Chief of the Imperial General Staff, had by his own description '*a happy brainwave*' and approached controversial armoured warfare specialist Major-General Percy Cleghorn Stanley Hobart to bring together Britain's experience and to develop new specialist armour for use on the beaches.

'*Hobo*' Hobart was a divisive character. General Wavell had forcibly retired him because of his unconventional ideas and, until quite recently, he had been serving as a lance-corporal in the Home Guard. Suddenly recruited by Brooke, Hobart's initial suspicion was that it was all some kind of trick, but he nevertheless got to work on radical new designs or '*Funnies*' for his unit, the 79th Armoured Division..

I

II

III

FUNNIES

I. DD DUPLEX TANKS

The DD Duplex tank was a converted M4A1 or M4A4 Sherman fitted with twin propellers and air-filled canvas floatation devices designed to '*swim*' to the beach from the invasion fleet. It would be released several miles out and make its own way in under its own power at a top speed of four knots. DDs were to be the only '*Funnies*' adopted by American forces on D-Day.

II. THE CROCODILE

A Churchill tank converted to carrying a flame thrower. Dragging around a tanker carrying 400 gallons of fuel, it was designed to assault blockhouses, pillboxes, trenches and strongpoints from a range of up to 360 feet. The fuel carried was enough for eighty one-second bursts. The flamethrower replaced one of the Churchill's machine guns, which meant that it could keep and use its main turret gun.

III. THE CRAB FLAIL

Both Shermans and Churchills could be converted to carry a mine flail, a spinning drum of forty heavy duty chains that flailed in front of the tank and set off any mines in its path. The tanks also kept their regular big guns and could be used to fight when not minesweeping.

IV. AVRE
(ASSAULT VEHICLE ROYAL ENGINEERS)

This Churchill conversion was armed with a Petard Spigot Mortar capable of firing a forty lb HE-filled projectile with a range of 500 feet. The projectile itself was nicknamed '*The Flying Dustbin*' — which it somewhat resembled. Hugely powerful, it was designed to demolish steel and concrete fortifications and obstacles — but the gunner had to clamber outside the protection of his tank to reload each time.

Other versions of the AVRE included the Bobbin (designed to lay down a carpet so that other armour could negotiate patches of soft sand), the Soft Box Girder (capable of laying down a thirty foot assault bridge over an obstacle in just 30 seconds) and the Carrot and Double Onion, both capable of planting heavy demolition charges against obstacles.

V. THE ARK

A Churchill conversion which could raise a ramp from its back, allowing other armour to drive up it and scale an obstacle.

IV

V

MULBERRIES

The Allies needed to capture at least one port for any invasion attempt to succeed — but the raid on Dieppe had proved that — even by 1942 — German port defences were just too strong to crack. Motivated minds were applied to the task and soon came up with an answer. The Allies would bring their own ports with them.

It was Vice-Admiral John Hughes-Hallett, the naval commander on the Dieppe Raid, who began to push for the creation of artificial harbours when he joined COSSAC. Lord Mountbatten requested that they needed to be at least one mile long and capable of serving ships of up to 2,000 tonnes.

The decision to use two artificial 'Mulberry' harbours — one American and one Anglo-Canadian — was taken at the Quebec Conference in August 1943. Each would handle up to 12,000 tons of supplies per day in the days following D-Day. Construction work began almost immediately at a large number of sites all over Britain. It was planned that on the afternoon of D-Day, they would begin their journey to the French coast at a stately 5 mph, pulled by tugs. Each harbour, when ready, would be equivalent to the size of Dover as a port.

I LIKE IKE

'(Eisenhower's) smile was worth twenty divisions.'

ADMIRAL MORTON DEYO, US NAVY.

On 7 December 1943, on his way back from the Cairo Conference, President Roosevelt summoned General Dwight '*Ike*' Eisenhower to a secret meeting in Tunis. There he told Eisenhower that he was going to command Operation Overlord. Eisenhower was somewhat surprised. There were more senior military men and he was disliked in some quarters for being too cautious and not battlefield-oriented enough. Also, both his parents were German. Nevertheless, Roosevelt had chosen him as Supreme Commander, Allied Expeditionary Forces, mainly because he got along with people. He liked the British, the British liked him, and he had already proven himself in battle beside them. Teamwork between the nations in the build up to D-Day would be nothing short of essential.

His deputy commander was to be Marshal Arthur Tedder of the RAF. General Bernard Montgomery would take overall charge of all ground forces (with General Omar '*Brad*' Bradley under him in charge of all American troops), while Air Marshal Trafford Leigh-Mallory of the RAF would be responsible for the air elements. Hero of Dunkirk Vice-Admiral Bertram Ramsay of the Royal Navy would take responsibility for the naval element. It came as no surprise that the overall commander was an American, but the appointment of four Britons to such high posts did raise a few eyebrows.

Eisenhower set up his SHAEF (Supreme Headquarters Allied Expeditionary Force) HQ in Bushy Park, within sight of Hampton Court Palace, got himself a little Scottie dog puppy for company — and almost immediately discovered that Montgomery had been revising the existing D-Day plans without his knowledge. Originally, D-Day was to have been fought with three Allied divisions. Montgomery wanted at least seven — two or three airborne divisions

followed by five more landing on the beaches to be followed by two more divisions in rapid succession. This panicked the navy element as they scarcely had enough landing ships and landing craft to meet the initial battle plan.

Eisenhower however liked Montgomery's thinking and was prepared to delay D-Day for an extra month to accommodate it. The target date was switched from 1 May to 1 June 1944.

THE PLAN

Montgomery was content with Normandy as the location for the invasion, but he wanted the attack to come along a front twice as large as that originally planned — totalling fifty miles instead of twenty-five.

Just after midnight on D-Day, three divisions of paratroopers and glider-borne troops would attack. The two American divisions — the 82nd and the 101st — would land on the Cotentin Peninsula to the west and the British 6th Division would land further east, broadly astride the River Orne. They would neutralise strongpoints, and assist the beach landings by either capturing routes off the beaches or else block German attempts to bring reinforcements to bear.

There would be five distinct invasion beaches running from Vareville in the west to Ouistreham in the east. Running west to east these were codenamed Utah, Omaha, Gold, Juno and Sword. The first two were to be taken by American units and Sword and Gold by the

OPP. PAGE: U.S. Army vehicles roll ashore on one of the floating causeways of the "Mulberry" artificial harbor off "Omaha" Beach, 16 June 1944

OPP. PAGE INSET: Lieutenant Commander R A Lochner, one of the designers of the Mulberry artificial harbour, working at Short Lake House, Weymouth, April 1944

RIGHT: General Dwight '*Ike*' Eisenhower

British. Juno would be the target of primarily Canadian units. The two American beaches would be attacked first, with the three more easterly beaches being assaulted approximately an hour later to allow for optimal tidal conditions. The attacks would be preceded by aerial bombardment and naval salvos from the warships. Following this, the British would bring in their 'Funnies' and engineers and help clear a safe path off the beach for both their DD armour and assault troops. The Americans, who had rejected the use of all 'Funnies' other than the DD tanks, would basically rely on their combat engineers alone to clear a way off the beach for the infantry. As a result, almost a quarter of the American force going ashore on D-Day would be combat engineers. For some reason, American commanders had chosen to 'charge the guns', beaching their landing craft directly in front of some of the most formidable German strongpoints. It is possible they thought that these would be smashed by the Allied bomber and naval assault — but the tactic was to have severe consequences.

The assaults would be performed by the American 1st, 4th and 29th Infantry Divisions, the British 3rd and 50th Infantry Divisions and the Canadian 3rd Infantry Division.

NEPTUNE

Operational Neptune, which was mostly the responsibility of the Royal Navy, covered the task of getting the troops to the landing beaches, supporting the landings and keeping the invasion forces supplied afterwards.

One hundred and thirty eight battleships, cruisers and destroyers were

BELOW L-R: British troops walking up the gangway of landing craft SS Empire Lance, on the way to France from Southampton; Taking a bearing on the ship's compass on board HMS Holmes whilst helping to guard the Allied supply lines to and from the Normandy beachhead; Two US Sailors stand at their gun aboard a Coast Guard-manned invasion transport on which they served during the invasion of Normandy

OPP. PAGE: Liberator bomber crews and pilots are briefed before setting off to bomb Germany and France

brought together to provide the initial bombardment before the troops went in, and to continue to provide artillery support during the big day. The British supplied the battleships Ramillies, Rodney and Warspite while the US Navy contributed the Arkansas, Nevada and Texas. Of the nineteen cruisers, the British supplied sixteen and the Americans three. Joining the fifty-seven Royal Navy destroyers and thirty American destroyers were a number from the Norwegian, Dutch, French and other foreign navies.

Altogether the military fleet would comprise a further 279 escorts, 287 minesweepers, 4 mine-layers, 495 motor boats, 310 landing ships and 3,817 landing craft. Adding to this ferries, tugs, ancillaries and merchant ships, and the total number of ships involved amounted to over seven thousand. Around seventy per cent of the vessels were either British or Canadian.

At the very heart of the operation were the landing craft and ships. They would need to be of many various sizes and designs to meet a range of needs. The big ships, like

the Landing Ship, Tanks (LSTs) were well over 300 foot long and capable of carrying dozens of tanks or other vehicles, as well as smaller landing craft. Landing Craft, Tanks (LCTs), on the other hand were just over 100 foot long and could carry up to eight tanks. Landing Craft, Infantry (LCIs) could carry almost 200 men. The basic infantry assault vehicle was the LCVP (Landing Craft, Vehicles and Personnel) or '*Higgins Boat*', capable of carrying a full platoon of men inshore from a mother ship.

AIR SUPPORT

Air power would play a vital role in the attack, both in the months leading up to D-Day and on the day itself. Achieving air superiority was considered key. If the Luftwaffe could strike in strength against the troops on the beaches or the ships out at sea, the invasion could very well fail. Fortunately for the Allies, the Luftwaffe was already chronically under strength in France, needing every spare aircraft to fight the Soviets on the Eastern Front or else defending German skies from Allied bomber fleets.

11,590 Allied aircraft would fly on D-Day, which would comprise the largest aerial operation in history. By contrast, the Luftwaffe could muster just 319 sorties and their effect on the invasion would be miniscule. It was calculated that the greatest danger to Allied warplanes on D-Day would be the chance of mid-air collision since there would be so many aircraft packing the same space, and friendly fire incidents. To try to prevent the latter, all aircraft taking part would have big thick black and white stripes, known as '*invasion stripes*' painted on them to aid identification.

Over 1,000 Transports, along with gliders, would deliver the three divisions of airbourne troops to their targets in France. Bombers would strike at radar stations to help prevent the advancing fleet from being detected, as well as at wide range of other targets including strongpoints and beach defences. They would be joined in striking ground targets by attack aircraft including the Typhoon and the Mosquito. Hundreds of squadrons of fighters would provide escorts to the bombers, or else cover Allied shipping and beach landings or act as aerial spotters for naval gunners.

THE ATLANTIC WALL

'The war will be won or lost on the beaches…We'll have only one chance to stop the enemy and that's while he's in the water, struggling to get ashore. The first 24 hours of the invasion will be decisive…for the Allies, as well as Germany, it will be the longest day.'

Field Marshal Erwin Rommel

From almost the moment America entered the war, the Germans accepted that the Allies would invade Europe. They also thought they knew exactly where the invasion would come — through the Pas de Calais. To the German mind, nowhere else was at all logical. The distance between Dover and Calais was just twenty-two miles and the quickest route would mean less danger and more chance of achieving surprise. Why would an invading army chooser a longer route ? The Allies would need to capture a port immediately — and the immediate area held not one but three major ports — Calais itself and then to the immediate east Boulogne followed by Dunkirk. An invading army coming through the Pas de Calais would also be almost perfectly placed for a race east to the Rhine, spilling over the bridges and into the Fatherland itself. So, the Pas de Calais it would be.

But they couldn't be certain.

Fuhrer Directive 40 in March 1942 instructed the German armed forces to begin the construction of an '*Atlantic Wall*' fortifying all the coastline from the Pyrenees to Holland — a stretch of over 3,700 miles. It would bristle with fortified strongpoints — 15,000 of them — and be defended by 300,000 soldiers. Work started in December 1942 but such were the pressures on Germany caused by war on the Eastern Front and the Allied bombing of the Reich itself that the project soon fell dismally behind schedule. By November 1943, Hitler was so concerned about the lack of progress on the Wall that he issued another Fuhrer Directive, declaring the lack of preparations in the West an emergency. Field Marshal Erwin Rommel was brought in to take personal charge of the defences. The elderly Field Marshal Gerd von Rundstedt would remain in overall charge of war in the west — but Rommel would report directly to the Fuhrer.

MAIN IMAGE: German 152 mm navy gun in bunker of the Batterie Le Chaos

BELOW L–R: Part of the Atlantic Wall being constructed; Several high ranking officers, including Makoto Onodera (Japanese Military Attaché to Sweden), visiting Fjell Fortress Circa1943; Northern France, Atlantic Wall, gun is being mounted to the bunker

LEFT: Stalin, Roosevelt& Churchill, outside entrance to building during the Tehran Conference

BELOW L-R: Fortitude decoy aircraft, tank & tankers

Rommel — who dreamed of being an engineer once the war was done — was horrified when he started his inspection of the existing fortifications. He denounced them as '*a figment of Hitler's Cloud Cuckoo Land.*' Only 30% of the work he expected to find had actually been done. There simply wasn't enough concrete available — and the hungry and brutalised slave labourers who comprised most of the 260,000 strong workforce, were hardly motivated. His soldiering experience told him that the strongpoints were all very well but what was needed were better defences on — and close to — the beaches. Immediately he started adding more minefields (or '*Devil's Gardens*') and barbed wire, more beach obstacles and nests of machine gun posts in between the strongpoints themselves. Inland, he ordered fields to be flooded to hinder paratroopers or the advance of invaders off the beach.

Rommel gave the most emphasis to the ports, especially those in the Pas de Calais, accepting that the Allies simply must seize a port. By May 1944 he had almost finished the work. Six and a half million mines were in place and half a million tank and landing craft obstacles were laid down. Units that were performing satisfactory were rewarded by Rommel with a free accordion.

There were sixteen thousand panzers ready for action in France and Belgium, including formidable Tiger tanks. Naturally, most of the armour was located close to the Pas de Calais area, where the invasion would be coming. Hitler, by now completely paranoid following at least six attempts on his life by members of his own army, insisted on having absolute and total control of the panzers. None could move without his personal permission.

There was only one panzer division in the area of Caen in Normandy, and two much smaller forces. The infantry in the Normandy area included a large number of Ost ('*East*') soldiers — mainly anti-communist Russians or Poles who volunteered to fight for Germany. Many more were youthful or elderly, sick or disabled in some way. The cream of Hitler's soldiery would be located closer to the Pas de Calais.

German resources were badly stretched. It was fortunate then that they knew the Allies would be striking at the Pas de Calais…

BODYGUARD, FORTITUDE & ZEPPELIN

'In wartime, truth is so precious that she should always be attended by a bodyguard of lies.'

Churchill, the Tehran Conference, Nov 1943

Somehow, the idea that the Allies might bring their own harbours with them never occurred to German planners. They continued to believe that the invasion would come at the Pas de Calais. The Allies knew this, and made every attempt to convince the Germans they were right. They also made every attempt to confuse them.

Operation Zeppelin was designed to try and convince the Germans that the real invasion would come through the Balkans and the '*soft underbelly of Europe*'. If it was to be believed, the Allies would launch a twin-pronged attack on Trieste and Greece, sweeping north to seize Rumania. The German High Command was never fully convinced by the tall tales spun by Zeppelin — but just in case, with typical thoroughness, they devoted twenty-five troop divisions to the region, divisions that could have otherwise been deployed to France.

Fortitude was a deception plan in three parts:

Fortitude North sought to convince Hitler that the Allies would storm Norway. Neutral Sweden would then join the war on the Allied side, allowing a massive Allied force to power south through Denmark and attack the Fatherland from the relatively unprotected North. To help the deception along, the Allies set up the HQ of an entirely fictitious '*British 4th Army*' in Edinburgh. In reality, it was little more than a room full of radio operatives. They in turn sent out transmissions to other similar rooms in Dundee and Stirling. The Germans quite naturally intercepted the messages — which included colourful information about rock climbing and cross-country skiing equipment — and were so taken in that they sent bombers to attack the force. German reconnaissance flights — which were deliberately not intercepted — reported back massed Allied aircraft on the Scottish airfields. In reality, these were wooden dummies. Germany asked its best secret agents to investigate. Both were now secretly working for the Allies and reported that there was indeed a genuine build up in the area. Norwegian resistance stepped up their attacks, British commandos raided with more frequency and German shipping off the Fjords was blitzed by RAF Bomber Command and Coastal Command. As a direct result of Fortitude North, a nervous Hitler committed a force of half a million troops along with tanks, big guns and aircraft, to defend Norway in the time leading up to D-Day.

Fortitude South was devoted to convincing Hitler that he was right in suspecting the Allies would attack at the Pas de Calais and sites further north in Belgium. At the heart of Fortitude South was the creation of the entirely fictional '*First US Army Group*', commanded by General George S Patton. Again, double agents confirmed its existence, while King George VI even paid it the honour of an official visit. Reconnaissance flights by the Luftwaffe spotted army camps ,

LEFT: Erwin Rommel

ABOVE L-R: Royal Air Force- 2nd Tactical Air Force; Preinvasion bombing of Pointe du Hoe by Ninth Air Force bombers; Daylight bombing raid on the railway yards at Tourcoing, France by aircraft of 2nd Tactical Air Force

landing craft in the ports and massed tanks in Kent. They even saw a large new oil refinery in Dover. None of it was real. It was created by, in part, special effects men from the British film industry and theatrical set designers. The massed Sherman tanks were just inflatable dummies and the landing craft shells of plywood and canvas. The oil refinery was courtesy of Britain's special effects wizards. Hitler, aware of 'Blood and Guts' Patton's reputation, became especially paranoid about the First US Army Group…

Fortitude South II (also called 'Rosebud') was largely a radio campaign intended to convince Hitler in the days after D-Day that the Normandy landings were just a diversion and the real attack would still come at the Pas de Calais. If Hitler fell for it (and he did), he would keep his main panzer force and precious 15th Army idling east of the Seine, still waiting for the anticipated 'real' Pas de Calais invasion even as the Allies took Normandy.

Hitler was totally convinced now: Invasion would come in three different, far flung places and he had to be ready for all of them.

Rommel, however, smelled a rat.

PREPARING FOR D-DAY

The planned Allied invasion of France, could not happen if the RAF and USAAF could not achieve total aerial superiority over the landing beaches. With that in mind, the RAF embarked on an ambitious programme of restructuring. No2 Group of Bomber Command — basically all their light and medium day bombers — were given over to Fighter Command in June 1943. Fighter Command itself was ended in November 1943, splitting into the 2nd Tactical Air Force (for use in Europe) and the Air Defence of Great Britain (which would comprise 10 day and 11 night fighter squadrons). The 2nd Tactical became part of the joint Allied Expeditionary Air Force, commanded by Air Marshal Trafford Leigh-Mallory.

In preparation for D-Day, the Allied Expeditionary Air Force pounded France for months with the intention of destroying the nation's transport infrastructure as part of 'The Transportation Plan'. Lancasters and Halifaxes hit Railway junctions and marshalling yards by night, while USAAF bombers pounded the same targets by day. They dropped 76,000 tons of bombs — the equivalent of three Hiroshima sized A-Bombs — on the railways. When the invasion came, it would prove difficult to ship reinforcements and materials in from Germany by rail or indeed to move assets around locally within northern France itself. The raids were very successful, with major damage done to France's railway network for minimal losses. In the last six weeks before D-Day it was estimated that 1,500 of the 2,000 steam locos of Region Nord had been destroyed. Attention then switched to radar stations, roads and bridges in the Normandy region and German-occupied airfields before finally switching to the coastal defences themselves.

In all the strikes, it was vital that the Germans couldn't tell the Allies' true area of interest. This meant hitting a lot of non-essential targets and almost right up until D-Day, four times the amount of bombs was dropped on the Pas de Calais area than around Normandy.

INFORMATION

The Government had been asking the British public to send in their holiday snaps of French coastal locations since 1942, and held a vast and eclectic reference library of some 10 million photos from which all manner of information might be gleaned.

The French resistance had been dutifully active in spying on German strongpoints and beach defences since the start of the Atlantic Wall project and were already providing invaluable information. Now, with the invasion nearing, they were asked to step up their efforts and responded fully. 50,000 French citizens joined in to provide information. Fighters noted the positions of hidden minefields by observing where German sentries did not walk. Ramblers out strolling carefully paced out the length of trenches or the distance between pillboxes. Some German units had deliberately removed their regimental markings to confuse details of their deployment, forgetting that every German soldier had his unit details sewn into his undies, which were sent to French laundries for cleaning. Resistance fighters amongst the washerwomen duly took note and sent the details on to London. Fishermen snapped pictures of the coast defences from the sea with hidden cameras . Railway clerks noted unusual troop movements. Waitresses listened to Germans idly chatting in cafes…

Above France, the Allies flew numerous photo reconnaissance missions, mindful not to pay too much attention to the Normandy area. Commandoes from COPP (Combined Operations Beach Reconnaissance and Assault Pilotage Parties) came ashore at night from midget submarines to take samples from beaches to find out whether or not the sand in the area could support the weight of armour.

All in all, by the time of D-Day, it was said with quiet confidence that the Allies knew more about the Atlantic Wall defences than the Germans did.

MAIN IMAGE: An American soldier is assisted by two French resistance men in pointing out German positions on a map

SOUTHWICK HOUSE

In early 1944, the advance command post of the Supreme Headquarters Allied Expeditionary Force was established at Southwick House, an elegant late Georgian-style manor house five miles north of Portsmouth. It was here that D-Day's top commanders would meet from now on to continue planning the invasion, living in camouflaged caravans or tents in the grounds. In quieter moments, it was not an uncommon sight to see Eisenhower and other senior figures enjoying a drink in the lounge bar of the Golden Lion public house in the local village of Southwick, which was now under strict lockdown.

HUSH

It was no mean feat to try and disguise one of the greatest military gatherings in history, but the Allies decided to give it a try.

Suddenly, as spring 1944 went on, all diplomatic travel in and out of Britain was abruptly ended. No diplomatic bags could be dispatched overseas. There was to be no more travel between Great Britain and neutral Eire: The German embassy in Dublin was known to have particularly big ears. Civilians were prevented from getting closer than ten miles to the south coast, in a swathe of secured land that stretched all the way from the Wash to Land's End. In Southwick Park, the two men who had installed the giant map showing the invasion plan were locked away under voluntary house arrest until D-Day. Staff were even forbidden to walk on the lawns in case spies or enemy aircraft spotted their footprints.

FORWARD

In May 1944, Britain sweltered in a heatwave. Temperatures of over 100 degrees Fahrenheit were not uncommon. The wind was still. The Channel as calm as a millpond. It was perfect weather for an invasion.

PRING...'

Across the last days of May and into the first days of June, men and machines in vast numbers started moving south through England. Seemingly endless fleets of ships brought in enlisted men from all corners of the British Isles. Railways thundered by day and night with troop or tank trains. Southern England was suddenly home to almost two million men. British and Canadian troops moved into Essex, Hampshire and Sussex, while American forces congregated further west in Dorset, Devon and Cornwall. Roads became quickly clogged. In Dorchester, civilian employees were given an extra 15 minutes for lunch — just to enable them to cross the road.

Everyone was heading south now into their designated assembly areas or '*sausages*' as they were known. Here, in huge tented and camouflaged encampments they were issued with grenades and ammunition, their lifejackets and new gas-resistant battledress (which the Americans called '*skunk suits*' on account of their foul smell). They were also given booklets full of advice on how to get on with the French. This included '*Don't mention 1940*', be wary of conmen charging vastly over-inflated prices and don't believe all you've heard about '*Gay Paree*'. They were also forbidden to talk to British civilians. The food — at least for the Americans — suddenly became better and new Hollywood movies were shown in special tents with free popcorn and candy bars. Whole libraries of new books appeared. — but no alcohol. Dance music played over camp loudspeakers. Men got issued with new rifles, and sharpened their bayonets and fought amongst themselves. A few shot themselves to escape to hospital or else went mad. Others shaved their heads or got a '*Mohican*' haircut. In Eisenhower's words;

'The mighty host was tense as a coiled spring.'

MAIN IMAGE: Britsh Landing Craft Wait For D-day. June 1944. Southampton

As of 1 June, all letters and phone calls out were forbidden. Troops received their final briefings on the most elaborate of table top dioramas. And Stars and Stripes magazine offered the GUIs some essential last minute advice;

'Don't be surprised if a Frenchman steps up and kisses you. That doesn't mean he's queer. It means he's French and darn glad to see you.'

From here soldiers would go by lorry or bus to their ships. The battleships, cruisers and destroyers started to sail too on the 2nd, from Belfast, Scapa Flow, the Clyde and other northern points, all heading to join the troop ships. The soldiers were all aboard by 2 June, playing cards, already feeling seasick and just waiting for the word that they were off. Verses of *'Why are we waiting?'* could be heard from Britons in ships all down the coast.

Ominously, all the hospitals on the south coast had been emptied of their patients, then meticulously cleaned and made ready. Fortunately, doctors now had access to Penicillin. German doctors didn't.

The heatwave had ended. It was raining now.

'The waiting for history to be made was the most difficult. I spent much time in prayer. Being cooped up made it worse. Like everyone else, I was seasick and the stench of vomit permeated our craft.'

Private Clair Galdonik, 359th Infantry Regiment

A STATE OF CONFUSION

At the same time as a great veil of secrecy descended over the British Isles, so Operation Fortitude stepped up their plans to confuse the Germans still further. Radio traffic to and from the (entirely fictitious) 1st Army suddenly increased dramatically. Fake lorry convoys raced around the south-east with a sense of real self-importance. Nazi Agents — all of whom had been successfully turned by British Intelligence — started reporting invasion dates and places — the Bay of Biscay on 15 June; the Pas de Calais sometime between 7-14 July. Someone

MAIN IMAGE: A soldier from 101st Light Anti-Aircraft Regiment (12th King's Regiment (Liverpool)) 3rd Division, prepares for D Day by reading at his French handbook at Camp A2 at Emsworth, near Portsmouth, Hampshire, 29 May 1944

even said that the invasion would come in Normandy between 5-7 June. Faced with a positive bombardment of contradictory information, German logic was just to ignore everything they were being told.

Come the beginning of June 1944, and the start of increasingly foul weather, the Germans were even more baffled as to why the invasion had not materialised. The weather during May had been perfect — warm, sunny, dry and still — and yet the Allies had not taken advantage. Cleverer minds among the German High Command began to suspect that the Allies would not come at all in 1944. They would bide their time and let Stalin do his worst on the Eastern Front. Perhaps the new improvements to the Atlantic Wall had deterred them and they would content themselves to take Italy.

Rommel did not share their increasingly relaxed attitudes. He knew something was wrong. The numbers, for one. The Americans and the British and their allies simply didn't have enough divisions for there to be a British 4th Army in Scotland poised to take Norway, a 1st Army in Kent to assault the Pas de Calais and who knew who in the Balkans region that was meant to take Rumania. The Germans were being played. It was now Rommel's instinct that the Allies would come in Normandy (although he was still baffled by the lack of a suitable port in the region). To stop the invasion even as it began he would need control of Hitler's prized panzers and move them on his own orders to Normandy.

Rommel made swift plans to have a personal meeting with Hitler to discuss a possible Normandy invasion. The date of the meeting was fixed for 6 June in Berlin. Rommel didn't mind leaving for Germany. It meant he could see his wife Lucie and give her a new pair of shoes and some flowers picked fresh from their garden for her 50th birthday (in the event, the shoes don't fit her). On 4 June, Rommel left France for Germany. It was now raining hard. Things were urgent but there was one thing he could be certain of — the Allies would never invade in this weather…

GO

On Saturday 3 June, SHAEF HQ got the news they had been dreading. Twenty-eight-year-old Group Captain Stagg appeared before the commanders at Southwick House with the latest weather forecast — and it was dire. The heat wave was over. Gone were the calm seas. Stagg appeared, one top RN officer recalled, like '*six feet two of Stagg and six feet one of gloom.*' The unhappy Scot told them that the Channel was going to be hit hard and heavy by ferocious storm conditions on 4 June — just as the landing craft would be setting out. Bad weather was expected to continue thereafter for the next three days, including thick low cloud around the paratrooper drop zones and even fog. Despite the ill-favoured weather, Eisenhower decided to order Force U and Force O to sail, just in case the weather improved. It didn't.

At 0600 the next day, Eisenhower very reluctantly took the decision to stop the invasion and to bring the ships back home. One part of the fleet, the one hundred and forty ships comprising Force U2A, failed to get the recall and carried on sailing unwittingly towards its intended target of Utah Beach with part of the US 4th Infantry on board. If it was spotted, the entire invasion might be in jeopardy. Force U2 was frantically chased down at sea by destroyers and a

Walrus aircraft and told to turn round, which it eventually did.

Eisenhower had to make a decision. Go again almost immediately, or wait for two weeks until the right conditions offered themselves up. The day of Sunday, 4 June, proved to be every bit as ferocious as feared. The Channel saw wild seas and the coastlines were assailed by high, ferocious waves and squalls of hard rain. Fierce wind and rain shook the windows of Southwick House. At 2100 on 4 June, Group Captain Stagg came to deliver the latest weather reports. He predicted that, in another 24 hours' time, there would be a short — and he meant short — period of more reasonable weather with lighter winds and calmer seas. This brief respite would last no longer than the evening of 6 June.

The officers of SHAEF broke up their meeting at midnight without making a final decision. They reconvened just four hours later after gathering their thoughts. Few were by nature gambling men, and to risk the success of the entire invasion on an unpromising and potentially unreliable weather prediction was a responsibility few relished — or even wanted. In the early hours, aware that time was now hard against them, they took a vote. Outside it was still raining. The vote was evenly split for and against, which meant Eisenhower himself would have to take the final

MAIN IMAGE: LCT craft on their way to the beaches during exercises in the English Channel, Portsmouth and Isle of Wight area to prepare for the Normandy landings

decision. The man known throughout the American High Command for his caution started to think. Some in the room swore later that the general had pondered for a good five agonising minutes before making his decision.

Eisenhower turned to face his officers. 'Ok,' he said. 'Let's go.'

Within just two hours, the first elements of the fleet was sailing out once more and the airborne divisions — who would be heading off to Normandy in just a few hours to comprise the first wave — finally got the word. Eisenhower tried to occupy himself by first watching the ships sail from Portsmouth and then by playing draughts. In his pocket was a letter of resignation in case D-Day was a failure. Elsewhere, General Patton was giving his (real) men a typically incendiary speech:

'We are advancing constantly and we are not interested in holding on to anything, except the enemy's balls. We are going to twist his balls and kick the living shit out of him…We are going to go through him like crap through a goose…'

SAILING

The Armada sailed now from ports all over the southern coastline, heading out into rough seas where violent gusts of wind whipped up waves five feet high. On the troopships, the men settled down to play cards, write one last letter home or throw up, while their officers received their final briefings. They rendezvoused at Area Z, twenty-five miles south of Portsmouth, which was so busy that the sailors thereafter referred to it as '*Piccadilly Circus*'. Coming out of Area Z under the cover of darkness , the ships would file south into one of five '*lanes*' each forty miles long and 400 yards wide. Into each went one task force — Force U bound for Utah Beach, Force O bound for Omaha, Force S for Sword, J for Juno and G for Gold. Closer in, those five lanes would become ten to allow the fast warships to get ahead of the slower transports.

Each task force sailed with minesweepers at their head. Few mines were found. The bombing of the French railways had delayed their shipping to the

ports. It was all coming together. On board British ships, men were being fed hearty meals of stew followed by plum pudding — if they could face it. A British destroyer played 'A-Hunting We Will Go' over its tannoy.

As the ships sailed on, coded messages were being sent out to the French Resistance. Among them were two lines of poetry;

'Blessent mon Coeur

D'une langueur Monotone'

'Wound my heart with a monotonous languor'. This meant the invasion was imminent and that the resistance should start to destroy German communications and sabotage the railways. (A member of German intelligence on the Belgian border had been warned by a collaborator to look out for this phrase, but when he tried to tell his CO, General Hans von Salmuth (CO of the 15th Army), he was summarily dismissed by the General with the immortal words '*I'm too old a bunny to get too excited about this.*')

The minesweepers reached their designated positions off Le Havre even before sunset on 5 June and kept well off. They were not spotted. German shipping and reconnaissance aircraft all sat in their bases, confident that the weather was too bad for an invasion to be heading straight for them. As a consequence, the Germans had only flown one reconnaissance flight over the Channel on the whole of 5 June — and that was up in Holland. The unthinkable had happened. No one knew they were there.

Waiting now offshore in the very early hours, the assault troops were fed

OPP. PAGE: American troops having loaded their equipment in LCT awaiting the signal to leave for the beaches

BELOW L-R: Major-General Richard Gale, GOC 6th Airborne Division, addresses his men, 4 — 5 June 1944; Men of 22nd Independent Parachute Company, 6th Airborne Division being briefed for the invasion; Men of No 4 Commando, 1st Special Service Brigade, marching from their assembly camp to Southampton for embarkation to Normandy, June 1944

another meal to fortify them through the fight ahead. On board American ships, the breakfast menu might include chicken, pork, steak, ice cream, donuts and candy bars. British troops tended to get a corned beef sandwich and a slop of rum. Most were by now so sick that breakfast was unthinkable. Everyone had been issued with travel sickness pills, but few soldiers took the medication because they knew it would make them drowsy — and a less than clear head was a good way to get killed in combat. On board the Prince Henry, the Canadian Scottish Regiment were provisioned with a packed lunch for the invasion comprising two hard boiled eggs and a cheese sandwich.

Back in England, CIGS Brooke wrote in his private diary:

"It is very hard to believe that in a few hours the cross Channel invasion starts. I am very uneasy about the whole operation. At the best it will fall so very far short of the expectation of the bulk of the people, namely all those who know nothing about its difficulties. At the worst it may be the most ghastly disaster of the whole war. I wish to God it were safely over.'

ADDRESS BY
GENERAL EISENHOWER

5 June 1944

'Soldiers, Sailors, and Airmen of the Allied Expeditionary Force:

You are about to embark upon the Great Crusade, toward which we have striven these many months. The eyes of the world are upon you. The hopes and prayers of liberty-loving people everywhere march with you. In company with our brave Allies and brothers-in-arms on other fronts you will bring about the destruction of the German war machine, the elimination of Nazi tyranny over oppressed peoples of Europe, and security for ourselves in a free world.

Your task will not be an easy one. Your enemy is well trained, well equipped, and battle-hardened. He will fight savagely. But this is the year 1944. Much has happened since the Nazi triumphs of 1940-41. The United Nations have inflicted upon the Germans great defeats, in open battle, man-to-man. Our air offensive has seriously reduced their strength in the air and their capacity to wage war on the ground. Our Home Fronts have given us an overwhelming superiority in weapons and munitions of war, and placed at our disposal great reserves of trained fighting men. The tide has turned. The free men of the world are marching together to victory.

I have full confidence in your courage, devotion to duty, and skill in battle. We will accept nothing less than full victory. Good Luck! And let us all beseech the blessing of Almighty God upon this great and noble undertaking.'

BRITISH AIRBORNE OPERATIONS

'Bring back as many of the chaps as you can.'

General Bernard Montgomery to Major John Howard, 5 June 1944

Codenamed Operation Tonga, the parachute drops and glider assaults by the men of the British 6th Airborne Division close to Caen on the night of 5-6 June had a number of different objectives. Using '*surprise, speed and dash*', they were to seize two vital bridges over the Caen Canal and the River Orne to allow passage for seaborne troops to advance inland from the beaches , while destroying a number of other bridges over the River Dives to stop German reinforcements moving up to attack the landings. Several key villages needed to be captured and held and — most important of all — the powerful German gun battery at Merville needed to be knocked out as it was believed to house a number of huge guns capable of bombarding Sword Beach on D-Day. After that the paratroopers were supposed to dig in and hold at all costs to defend the left flank of the invasion until they could be relieved by troops advancing inland off the beaches. A ferocious counterattack by the 21st Panzer Division was expected.

First in were plywood Horsa gliders holding six platoons of the 2nd Battalion, Oxford and Buckinghamshire Light Infantry, commanded by Major R J Howard. None of his men had ever fought before. They had been towed over to France by Halifax bombers. At 0015, the tows were slipped at 5,000 feet, freeing the gliders before the fully laden Halifaxes went on to bomb Caen.

The lead assault glider touched down in the moonlight just 47 yards from the eastern end of the bridge over the canal, codenamed Pegasus Bridge. It came down hard, breaking its nose, knocking the two pilots unconscious and ending

up swathed in ripped up coils of barbed wire. The men made their exit through the shattered cockpit and at once started their assault on the bridge, more gliders landing (or crash landing) all around them. In the second glider, pilot Oliver Boland issued the instruction, '*we're here. Piss off and do what you're paid to do*' to the still-shaken soldiers. The glider had landed slap on top of a German trench and there were German soldiers tangled up in the shattered wooden frame, all eager to surrender.

Spotting the glider troops racing towards them , a sentry on the near side of the bridge fled, shrieking a warning. Another sentry on the far side then sounded the alarm. A burst from the Sten gun of twenty-six year old Lieutenant

Den '*Danny*' Brotheridge silenced him but, as the German defenders tumbled *into their pillbox and trench system, Brotheridge took a bullet through the throat. He was to be the first Allied fatality on D-Day. His wife Margaret was eight months pregnant. The shaken and only half-awaken German soldiers were routed and captured very quickly. Pegasus Bridge was taken. Half a mile to the east, other platoons had landed and seized the bridge over the Orne. It turned out to be undefended. The signal went out — Ham and Jam' — meaning that both bridges were now in British hands. Now the British troops had to hold the bridges — and German reinforcements were certain to be on way.*

Just as the bridges were being taken, 620 men of the 5th Parachute Brigade were jumping from converted Stirling bombers. Low cloud had made navigation difficult, which meant the thirty-three Stirlings had to circle to get their bearings on the drop zone. This inevitably attracted the attention of the German flak batteries below and they

MAIN IMAGE: '*Pegasus Bridge*' over the Caen Canal at Benouville, Two of the Horsa gliders that brought the 2nd Battalion in on the night of D-Day can be seen in the background

ANGELS WITH
DIRTY
FACES.

MAGARET
JOYCE.
MARGIE
KATH
OLIVE
ELSIE

opened up. Two Stirlings were hit and plunged into the ground killing the crews and the paratroopers trapped aboard. The rest released their paratroopers at 0050, scattering them considerably. Some fell up to twelve miles away from the target. The men came down with tracer bullets streaking around them — and then once on the ground began the tricky tasks of joining up with others. Commanding the 5th on this operation, Lieutenant Colonel Richard Pine-Coffin was initially as confused about his location as his men. Once he gathered his bearings though, he started to rally them. An Aldis lamp was used to mark his position, while someone repeatedly blew a hunting horn. By 0215 Pine-Coffin had managed to call in 250 of his 620 men and decided that had to be enough. They could hear shooting coming from the captured bridges and knew they were needed. What there was of the 5th took up pre-arranged positions around the bridges and dug in. They were only lightly armed with their own personal weapons. Their mortars and medium machine guns had all gone missing in the jump. Now they expected to have to fight off German armour.

The men of the 12th Battalion had jumped from their Stirlings with the aim of seizing Le Bas de Ranville under the command of Lieutenant-Colonel A. P. Johnson. Like the 5th, they found themselves scattered all over the area and it took until 0200 before Johnson mustered enough men to feel confident of taking his target. On the way, they ambushed a motorcyclist and an armoured car, which just happened to contain the German officer responsible for the area. He had been on his way to see some prostitutes and was laden with gifts which included the scraps of his own luxurious dinner.

OPP. PAGE: Airborne troops prepare to fly out as part of the second drop on Normandy on the night of 6th June 1944

BELOW L-R: Paratroops of 6th Airborne Division blackening their faces in front of an Albemarle aircraft at RAF Harwell, 5 June; Transport moving across the Caen Canal Bridge at Benouville; Members of 12th Parachute Battalion, 5th Parachute Brigade, 6th Airborne Division, enjoy a cup of tea after fighting their way back after three days behind enemy lines, 10 June

Landing next to the 12th, the 13th Battalion had suffered badly in the drop. Half of them had come down in a heavily wooded area. Many had sustained injuries and the Germans had shot a number as they desperately tried to free themselves from entanglement in the trees. Those who did land at the drop zone were successfully mustered by the sound of hunting horns and ploughed on regardless, taking bridges over the Orne and Dives and clearing the vicious anti-glider poles in the nearby cornfields for the next wave of gliders to come down in. One of the Dives bridges was destroyed when a British sergeant simply sauntered up to it unchallenged, nonchalantly laid his explosives and detonated them from a distance. Another, considered the most important of all five, was only destroyed after Major J D A Roseveare commandeered a medical jeep, packed it full of explosives and then drove hell for leather through the German-occupied village of Troarn with a few men and a Bren gunner perched in the back laying down covering fire as tracers flew overhead. The jeep made it to the bridge but the gunner didn't. He was shot and fell from the vehicle as they went. Reaching the bridge, Roseveare and his surviving men with him destroyed it before they ran off and hid from the

OPP. PAGE: Overhead aerial of the gun battery at Merville (3km east of Ouistreham) consisting of four medium casemates, after air bombardment, c. May 1944

Germans in the village, eventually falling fast asleep in woodland.

The seventy-two supply gliders duly came at just after 0300, separating from the aircraft towing them at 2,500 feet and already taking anti-aircraft fire. Some landed virtually unscathed. Others were torn and holed, or tipped upside down. One smashed into a farmhouse. Others ended nose down and tail up. There was no time to recover from the shock of the brutal landings. Those who could extricated themselves from the gliders and came pouring out into the moonlit cornfields. Some advanced to form a defensive perimeter while others started to unload precious cargo. It was a distinct relief for the men to find that ten of the eighteen anti-tank guns had survived the landings. When the heavy equipment had been unloaded, the men moved off to link up with the 12th and 13th at Ranville.

The 1st Canadian Parachute Battalion experienced severe difficulty when they started dropping after 0100. Their pilots two became confused between the River Dives and the Orne (which were just five miles apart)and also flew well off course as they tried to avoid increasingly thick anti-aircraft fire. A number of parachutists ended up falling into the Dives or the flooded areas around it and were drowned, pinned to the bottom by their heavy equipment. All told, Canadian paratroopers were scattered over an area forty times the size of the intended drop zone. Despite this, the Canadians succeeded in destroying all five of the bridges over the Dives they were ordered to deal with.

THE MERVILLE BATTERY

One of the most important objectives assigned to British Airborne forces was the destruction of the Merville Battery. The battery was thought to contain four massive 150mm guns inside thick concrete casemates that posed a serious threat to the British troops due to land on Sword Beach in just a few hours' time. Merville was defended by 210 German troops, ten machine gun nests and three thick fields of barbed wire separated by two mine fields.

The assault on Merville began with a special reconnaissance party dropping earlier than the main force to mark the dropping zone and to scout ways through the formidable defences to allow the troops to get at the guns. To do

this meant poking the dirt for mines with their fingertips…

Just after half past midnight, a force of one hundred heavy RAF Lancaster bombers attacked the Merville battery to soften it up — but missed. Due to the low cloud, the Lancasters unloaded their 4,000 lb bombs a good half mile off target, almost hitting the reconnaissance party in the process.

Now came the main assault force, their aircraft hunted by searchlights and battered by anti-aircraft fire. Like other pilots that night, the airmen flying them in also became confused by the two rivers. As a result, the force dedicated to assaulting Merville tumbled from their planes in a state of complete chaos. They were all meant to land in a neat drop zone a mile long by one and a half miles wide. Instead, they became scattered over an area of hostile territory comprising some 50 square miles. Some were so far off they landed in with the Americans. Almost two hundred simply vanished and have not been found to this day. To add to the disaster, all five of the raider's equipment gliders carrying their jeeps and anti-tank guns were lost in a wild storm over the Channel.

The man assigned to lead the attack on Merville, twenty-nine-year old Lieutenant-Colonel Terrence Otway, came parachuting in with the main force — and landed directly on top of an old farmhouse which was serving as a German headquarters. Once they had recovered from the shock, the German officers fired on him with their side arms. Luckily, Ordway's batman had landed nearby and flung a stone through the window of the house. The Germans inside fled, thinking it was a grenade and Ordway and his Batman escaped, aided by some very lost Canadian paratroopers who had seen them come down.

Otway now had to make a decision. He could only find 150 of his men out of 650 in total, and he had lost all of his heavy equipment. Attacking the battery would surely be suicide, but Otway decided to press on regardless towards Merville through the country lanes with what he had.

On the edge of the battery, the paratroopers met up with their reconnaissance party who had already cut holes in the wire and marked a way through the minefields with the heels of their boots. They had also tried to determine where all the German sentries were located. Otway led his men silently through to the inner wire. Zero hour was 0430. What Otway was waiting for was the sudden appearance of three gliders packed with troops and demolitions experts that were due to land right on top of the Merville battery, achieving total surprise. In reality one of the

OPP. PAGE: American paratroopers attached to the static line just prior to jumping during the invasion of Normandy

three gliders had already been lost. Its tow rope had snapped shortly after take-off and the glider was forced to come down in England. Now though, the surviving two gliders were coming in. The anti-aircraft gunners at Merville started blasting away at them as their tug planes circled in some confusion. The paratroopers below were meant to mark the drop zone with star shells — but they'd all been lost in the drop so no signal could be given. The gliders were released nevertheless on a best guess basis. In the heat of the moment, one of the glider pilots confused the village of Merville with the battery and set his men down just outside the hamlet — a good four miles away. The one remaining glider came down close to target, taking ferocious fire which incapacitated a number of those on board. As he came in, the pilot chose a target field only to see a sign saying '*Achtung! Minen!*' at the last minute. Somehow he managed to bring the nose of his glider up, clear the field, hop a lane and come down in the next field over. The survivors tumbled out as the glider smouldered and then caught fire.

All German attention turned to the glider troops. No one had yet spotted Otway's men inside the wire. Ten machine gun nests opened fire. Otways' sole Vickers gun blew away three of them in rapid succession. At the same time, Otway's troops detonated Bangalore torpedoes, blowing a hole through the last remaining barbed wire. Advancing, the British raiders split into two parties — one targeting the German machine gun nests while the other went directly for the big guns. Reaching the massive concrete structures housing the guns, they were stunned to find that the Germans had just left the back doors open. The party fired everything they had into the casemates and the surviving Germans were soon streaming out to surrender. The paratroopers poured in to get at the guns — only to discover that they were not 150mm as expected but smaller 75mm guns. All four were quickly wrecked, a job overseen by Lieutenant M. Dowling, who confirmed that the last gun was out of action before dying of his wounds.

The attack on the Merville Battery was undertaken successfully in just twelve minutes. Otway ordered a flare to be sent up from a Very pistol, telling the ships gathered offshore that the Merville Battery had been neutralised and that there was no need to shell it. They had taken Merville with just fifteen minutes to spare before the naval salvo was due to hit it. One of his signals officers also released a homing pigeon — which had somehow survived

safely inside the man's battledress and sent it back to London with news of the victory. Of the one hundred and fifty men who had taken part in the assault on the Merville battery, a full 50% were now casualties. Just twenty-two of the Germans manning the battery survived the fierce action to become prisoners.

Later in the day, as Otway and his men were leaving Merville, they would be mistaken for German troops and attacked by USAAF aircraft. After the war, Otway would go on to run a toyshop in Knightsbridge.

AMERICAN AIRBORNE OPERATIONS THE 82ND AIRBORNE

The US 82nd Airborne Division — the '*All-Americans*' — had been officially activated on 16 August 1942. All the men were volunteers and all were expected to fit the job description of being '*lean and mean.*' The Division had previously been used in the invasion of Sicily, but their drop there had not been a success. Hundreds of men had fallen into the sea and been killed and those who did land on the island itself were so scattered that, out of the 3,400 who dropped, their commanding officer could only find twenty of them five hours into the invasion. The Sicily drop had given Eisenhower some sleepless nights about how the 82nd might perform in Normandy…

The objective of the 82nd in the early hours of 6 June, under the command of Major-General Matthew Ridgeway, was to drop near the Merderet River. From there, some forces were to clear the area west of the river while others were to move east and seize the market town of St. Mere-Eglise along with the crossroads nearby where roads ran off to Cherbourg — and straight down to Utah Beach. Once taken, they were to destroy bridges over the Douve River, capture some bridges over the Merderet, prepare landing grounds for gliders bringing in heavy equipment and then hold their positions against any German counter-attack launched against Utah Beach from the north west later that day.

Before the main force landed, special pathfinders teams went in to mark the drop zone. Their planes encountered low cloud coming in and became disorientated. The pilots had not been trained for bad weather — or night flying for that matter. Fewer than 40 per cent of the C-47s employed for the American drop had navigators on board and the pilots were forced to make

OPP. PAGE: Major-General Matthew Ridgeway

BELOW L–R: Douglas C-47 Skytrain USAF; C-47 Internal view; General James Gavin

snap decisions about their locations, often while under anti-aircraft fire. All too often they got it wrong. Virtually all of the Pathfinder teams were dropped in the wrong location. One team was dropped over the Channel and drowned. Of the eighteen American Pathfinder teams deployed only one made it to its designated drop zone and was able to complete its mission.

The 6,420 men of the 82nd following them in aboard 430 C-47s had no idea of what had happened to their Pathfinders. They took off on Operation Boston from airfields around Nottingham fifty minutes after the Pathfinders in ten waves. Each man had to be helped into his C-47 transport because of the sheer weight of the equipment he was carrying. The waves of C-47s — each carrying fourteen to eighteen men — crossed the Channel at 500 feet, rising up to 1500 feet over the Channel Islands to avoid the AA batteries before dropping to 600 feet again for their run in to Normandy. A naval officer watching the formations go overhead described them silhouetted against the light of the full moon as '*like groups of scudding bats*'.

A lower drop height was intended to bring the paratroopers down quicker, saving valuable seconds in the air where they were vulnerable to being machine gunned from the ground. The height proved impractical when the first wave flew straight into a totally unexpected thick fog bank. To avoid collisions,

the tight transport formation began to break up and disperse. Emerging from the clouds, the low flying C-47s immediately met a hail of anti-aircraft fire from the ground, with everything from 88 shells to small arms fire being directed against them. Some transports blew up in mid-air. Others, their engines on fire, tipped and went into the ground, exploding in a fireball.

The sudden fierce anti-aircraft fire disconcerted many of the pilots. Most had no previous combat experience and certainly no experience of flying through ground fire at low level. They were meant to slow down to 90 mph for the drop, but now that was looking increasingly like suicide. Instead they gave in to their instincts and sped up. Back with the troops, red lights started switching to green — the signal to jump. Paratroopers began to plummet from the formation into the darkness. In the Chaos, virtually no one jumped where they were supposed to be. Some jumped too low and never had a chance for their parachutes to open. One paratrooper who had landed safely saw every man jumping from a low-flying C-47 simply fall and hit the ground. They sounded, he said, like '*watermelons falling off the back of a truck.*'

As they jumped, many lost the 80lb of extra equipment hanging in special packs from their legs. They simply snapped and the equipment was lost. German troops on the ground fired flares and then directed fire up against the descending paratroopers who were now starkly illuminated. Thirty-six men fell into the deliberately flooded areas around the Merderet River and drowned in four feet of filthy water because they could not get rid of their heavy packs. Much of the 82nds heavy equipment was also lost in the waters. Only 4% landed in their assigned drop zones. Some fell so far afield that they ended up

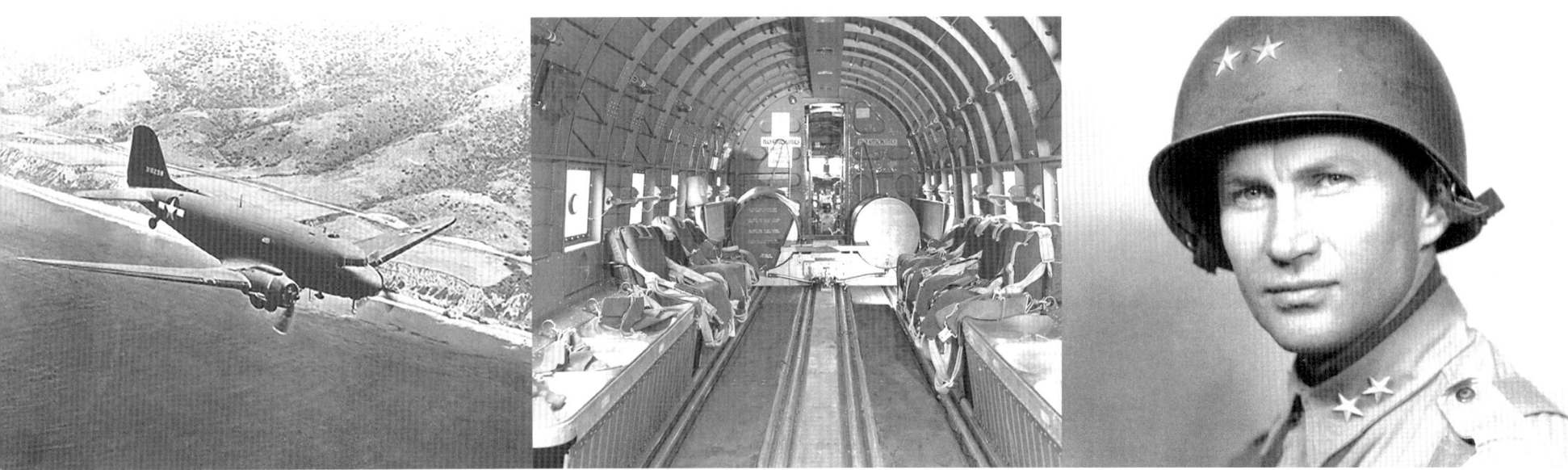

in the drop zone allocated to the 101st and ended up fighting alongside them. Three days after D-Day, 4000 men of the 6,420 men of the 82nd were still missing and unaccounted for.

The man in charge of taking St. Mere-Eglise, General James Gavin, was fortunate in being able to find twenty of the men who jumped with him within an hour. They were completely lost. Gavin sent out patrols, who found their position — and a number of other stragglers too. In total, Gavin had a band of 150 men when he set out, armed only with their personal weapons. Everything else was lost in the dark.

Meanwhile, two platoons of the 505th Regiment of the 82nd had landed directly on top of St. Mere-Eglise itself. Unfortunately for them, despite it being the early hours of the morning, the entire village was awake — along with the German garrison. A building in the old cobbled town square had caught fire and everyone was up and about forming bucket chains to try and dowse the flames. Into the chaos dropped the first American paratroopers. A German machine gun post in the church bell tower opened up, cutting a bloody swathe through the descending men. One paratrooper simply came apart in the air when a round hit his grenades and another fell directly into the burning building. The men landing in the village square were swiftly gunned down by the Germans before they could even shed their parachutes and the men tangled up in trees and telegraph wires suffered a similar fate. One paratrooper, Private John '*Buck*' Steele, came down directly on the church bell tower and was snagged. He hung there for the entire battle, playing dead as the fighting raged around him, until some Germans decided to loot his body for cigarettes and chocolate. They found him very much alive and took him prisoner. Incredibly, the fighting now over, the German garrison elected to go to bed. They were rudely awakened by more men from the 505th, who had fallen just outside St. Mere-Eglise, being directed straight to their billets by bloodthirsty French Patriots. Ten died resisting. A further thirty surrendered in a daze. By 0430, St. Mere Eglise was in American hands — just.

Scattered and away from the main objectives, hundreds of individuals and little groups fought small guerrilla actions throughout the night. In one, General Wilhelm Falley, Commanding officer of the crack 91st Germany Infantry Division, was ambushed and killed in his staff car by Lieutenant Malcolm Brannen of the 82nd.

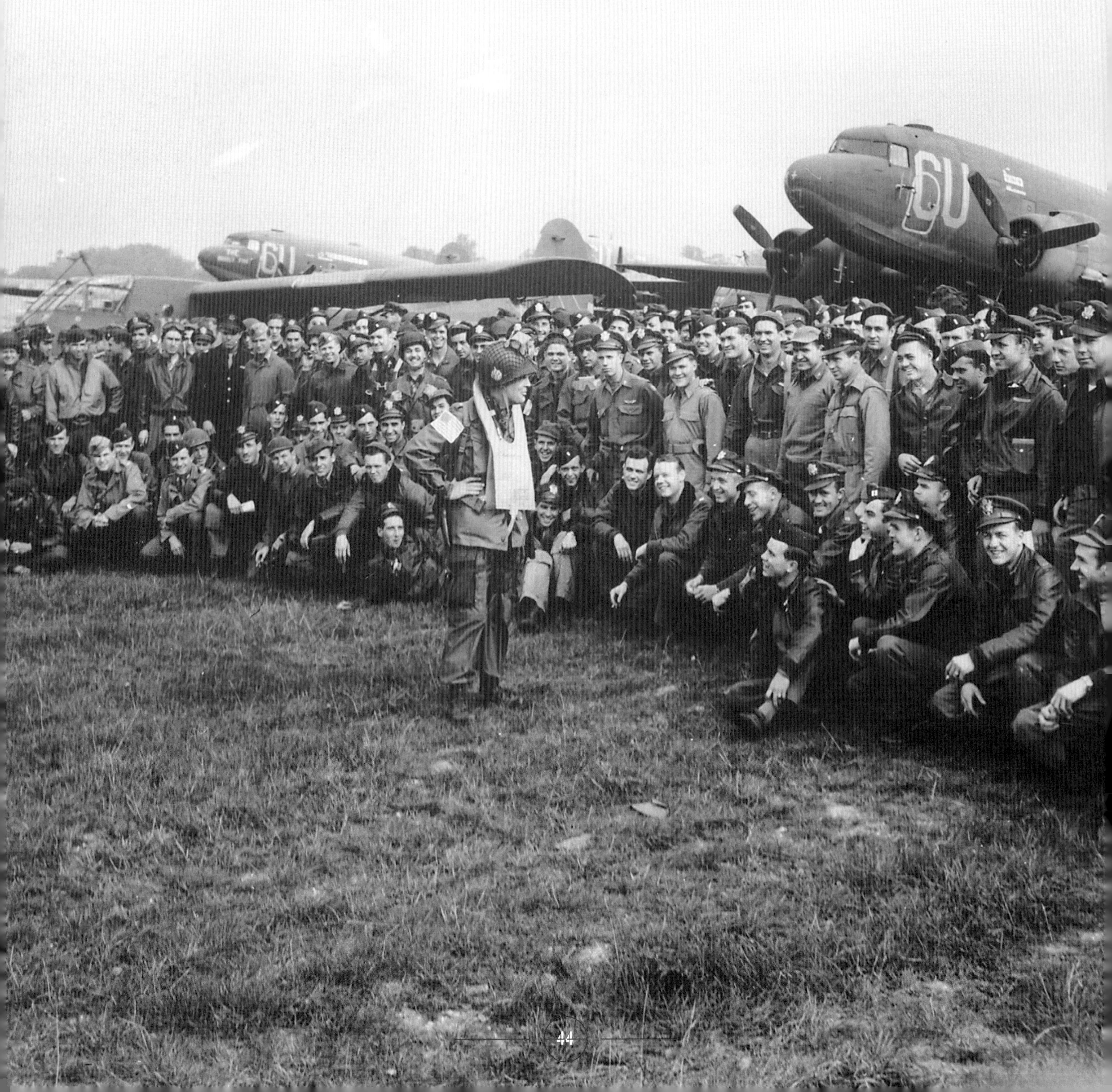
6U
6U

The drop had been so chaotic and the resistance encountered so strong that the paratroopers had had little if any time to seize and prepare the landing grounds for the fifty-two Waco supply gliders comprising Operation Detroit — but they came in anyway at dawn, swooping in on Hiesville, close to St. Mere-Eglise, bearing jeeps and 57mm anti-tank guns as well as 957 reinforcements. The landing was a rough one, under heavy anti-aircraft fire. The hedges in the Bocage proved far higher and tougher than regular hedgerows in England. Some gliders slammed into them and broke or were brought up short. Others hit houses or came down in woods and just fell apart, spilling out men and heavy equipment. Some ended up nose down and tail in the air. The strain of landing then tore the heavy equipment being carried away from their straps and it tumbled forward, crushing the pilots to death. Other pilots died impaled on jagged plywood shafts from their own gliders. One came down directly on a land mine. Twenty five paratroopers died in the landings and a further 118 were injured. Nineteen of the 111 jeeps being transported were wrecked, as were four of the seventeen precious anti-tank guns.

The 82nd achieved few of their objectives. They had taken St. Mere-Eglise, but the position was far from secure and was still under siege from German artillery three days later. None of the bridges over the Douve were destroyed, nor any of the bridges over the Merderet captured. Casualty figures for the 82nd on D-Day were estimated as 20% — or some 1,260 men killed, wounded or missing. While they might have failed in most objectives however, the men of the 82nd — and the 101st — did succeed in causing the Germans no little confusion, and the German response to them attracted attention and valuable fighting resources inland and away from the beaches.

OPP. PAGE: Brigadier General Anthony C. McAuliffe, artillery commander of the 101st Airborne Division, gives his various glider pilots last minute instructions before the take-off

BELOW L-R: Eisenhower addresses American paratroopers prior to D-Day; Paratroopers of the 377th, 3/502th, 506th and 508th Parachute Infantry Regiment of the 101st Airborne Division in Marmion Farm at Ravenoville, Utah Beach; Among the first to make successful landings, holds a Nazi flag captured in a village assault. Marmion Farm at Ravenoville, Utah Beach

AMERICAN AIRBORNE OPERATIONS
THE 101ST

'Before the dawn of another day, I'll sink this knife into the heart of the foulest bastard in Nazi Land!'

Colonel Howard 'Jump' Johnson, in a pep talk to 501 PIR, 5 June 1944

If there were serious concerns that even an experienced division like the 82nd Airborne would not be able to cope with the demands of their D-Day drop, then there were even greater fears for the efficacy — and safety — of the 101st Division. Nicknamed 'The Screaming Eagles', the 101st had been activated at the same time as the 82nd but had not yet been tested in combat.

OPP. PAGE: Major-General Maxwell Taylor

MAIN IMAGE: U.S. Army Air Forces Douglas C-47A Skytrain, tow Waco CG-4A gliders during the invasion of France in June 1944

Under the new command of Major-General Maxwell Taylor, the 101st were to drop west and north of the 82nd and assigned the task of seizing the four main roads and causeways leading off Utah beach, holding them for the troops who would be storming Utah in just a few hours' time. They were also to destroy a German coastal artillery battery at Saint-Martin-de-Varreville, capture bridges over the Douve River and destroy some road bridges.

Airsickness was rife on board the C-47s of the 9th US Airforce Troop Carrier Squadron taking the men over, so much so that the floors of the planes were described as slick and slippery. Despite this, Major-General Taylor made a show of putting down a pillow on the floor then lying down and catching a nap during the journey over. The message to his men was that there was nothing to worry about. History does not record whether he was vomited over during his nap. It does record however that his men had great difficulty waking him up again, whereupon he insisted on being the first out of the door.

If the 82nds drop was near disastrous, then the 101sts was even worse. Jumping between 0048 and 0140, they suffered many of the same difficulties as the 82nd. Their planes hit unexpected fog and cloud, scattering their

formations. Many planes lacked navigators. Inexperienced pilots encountering serious flak took hard evasive action, flying too fast and dropping their men at the earliest opportunities rather than on time. As a result, the 101st simply came apart as a cohesive unit even as the men dropped, being scattered widely across twenty-five miles of hostile French countryside.

The men of the 101st experienced much the same as those of the 82nd as they dropped, a sky full of tracer fire and treacherous marshlands below in which a heavily laden man could drown. Heavy equipment and weapons simply disappeared beneath the waters. Some fell in the sea. Some were so far away they did not see a friendly face again until D-Day+23. Lieutenant-Colonel Louis Mendez found himself an incredible 90 miles from his drop zone. He walked there in five days, killing six Germans en route. Even several days after D-Day, the 101st could only call upon 1,000 of the 6,000 men who had dropped.

Virtually all of the men of the 2nd Battalion, 502nd Parachute Infantry Regiment were dropped in the wrong place. Only its commander, Lieutenant-Colonel Steve A. Chappuis and the men from his plane came down in their allotted drop zone. Undaunted, they duly marched to their target, the artillery battery at Saint-Martin-de-Varreville. They found it — only to discover that the Germans had already dismantled it and sent the guns elsewhere.

Major-General Maxwell Taylor found himself completely alone and disorientated for the first twenty minutes on the ground. When he finally

located his first paratrooper, the general threw off all decorum and gave him a huge hug. As they tried to get their bearings, the pair were joined by other confused stragglers. Taylor ended up in charge of a rag-tag group comprised of two generals, four colonels, four lieutenants, some NCOs and just a dozen ordinary fighting men. '*Never have so few been commanded by so many,*' he wryly commented later. The men eventually found themselves at one of the objectives — a causeway off Utah Beach. They improvised an attack plan and successfully took the causeway. The planners had allowed 1,200 men for the job. Taylor took it with 150.

Also collecting men was Colonel Howard Johnson, who managed to round up 150 paratroopers and seized another of the 101st's primary objectives, the lock on the Douve at La Barquette at 0400. They were soon reinforced by a nearby glider drop codenamed Chicago and comprising fifty-one Waco gliders carrying 150 reinforcements and serious anti-tank guns. Just as with the 82nd, many of the gliders were wrecked on landing and the assistant commander of the 101st, Brigadier-General Donald Pratt, was amongst the fatalities having broken his neck on impact.

Lieutenant-Colonel Robert Ballard rounded up 250 lost paratroopers and led them towards Sainte Côme-du-Mont to destroy some road bridges over the Douve but was blocked half a mile from his objective by fierce resistance from German paratroopers. The defenders were also attacked by an impromptu force led by Major Richard J. Allen, but managed to fight them off too and hold the bridge.

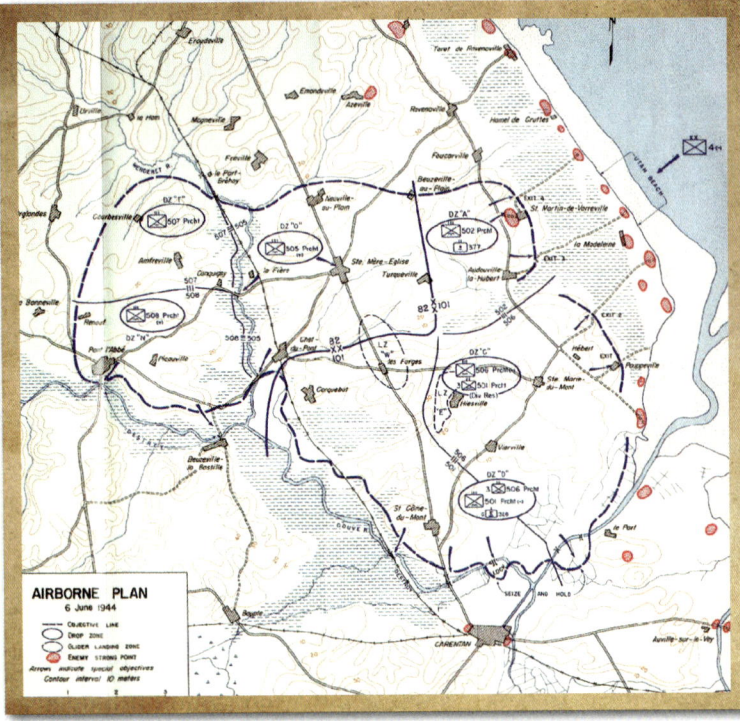

AIRBORNE PLAN
6 June 1944

OBJECTIVE LINE
DROP ZONE
GLIDER LANDING ZONE
ENEMY STRONG POINT
Arrows indicate special objectives
Contour interval: 10 meters

OPP. PAGE: Trolleys loaded with 500-lb GP and MC bombs, and their attendant armourers, are towed by tractors from the Bomb Store to the awaiting Handley Page Halifaxes of No. 51 Squadron RAF which were operating in support of the Allied Armies in Normandy

LEFT: Map of Planned airborne drop zones, D-Day, 6 June 1944

Below L–R: A U.S. Army Air Force Waco CG-4A-WO glider; Mitchell Mark II, of No. 98 Squadron RAF based at Dunsfold, Surrey, unloading its bomb load over a flying-bomb launching site in northern France; Low-level oblique aerial photograph showing the heavily-bombed flying-bomb assembly and launch bunker at Siracourt, France

Captain Charles Shettle of the 506th PIR assembled a platoon-sized group of men and took two-foot bridges over the Douve near la Porte at 0430. They crossed the bridges but ran low on ammunition after assaulting several German machine gun nests and had to withdraw to the nearside of the bridges. Here they held, being joined by more and more stragglers attracted by the sound of gunfire. Isolated they were forced to hold — and fight — throughout D-Day.

Elsewhere, two battalions of the 506th managed to collect themselves and

started in for the rear of what would be, in just a few short hours, Utah Beach. Vital roads were seized and Pouppeville was stormed. In fierce house to house night fighting, the paratroopers drove the Germans out in a battle lasting three full hours.

Away from the 101st's objectives, the true story of the night was that of thousands of lost men wandering around behind enemy lines in almost pitch darkness, relieved only by moments when moonlight managed to penetrate the low cloud ceiling. Some used their initiative and tried to sever telephone lines they came across to impede and confuse German communications. Others found a safe place and hid. Virtually none of them had any idea where they were — and as one or two started to meet up, rumours began to

spread of Nazi atrocities. Paratroopers hanging from trees had been used for bayonet practice or turned into human torches by Nazis with flamethrowers. Helpless and wounded American prisoners had been machine gunned by the SS. One paratrooper came across the bodies of two men of the 101st with their genitals cut off and placed in their mouths. After that, his commanding officer told him to take no prisoners. It was true that the Germans had committed a number of atrocities that night. They had been told that American paratroopers were all part of a penal division made up of convicted murderers, rapists, slum-dwellers and gangsters — and as a result many German soldiers were simply terrified of them. They needed to be killed.

As a result of the rumours of atrocities, a number of the lost American paratroopers elected to go 'Kraut Hunting', whether alone or in small groups. That would be their contribution to the night. Some watched for the tracer fire that gave away German machine gun positions. Paratroopers would then creep up on them and deposit grenades over the sandbags. Other

German prisoners were executed, supposedly in revenge. One man was caught the next morning with a ghastly necklace made from an old bootlace threaded through the severed ears of the Germans he'd killed over the course of the night. For most of the men, the savagery of 'Kraut Hunting' was a spontaneous response to being scared and lost, all alone in the dark.

IN THE AIR TONIGHT

In addition to the paratrooper and glider attacks, other operations were being carried on throughout the Normandy area and beyond.

1,136 aircraft from RAF Bomber Command pounded targets far and wide, some of them relevant to the forthcoming landings, others purely diversionary, while others dropped over 2,000 SOE agents and SAS troopers into France.

Some had instruction to meet up with local French resistance groups and lead them on special missions. Others had targets that they would attack by themselves or just '*do little bits of killing here and there.*' Radar stations were attacked all along the invasion coast. As the invasion fleet came in, only nine were still in operational order. The Luftwaffe, such as it was, spent the night chasing '*ghost signals*' over Amiens created by RAF bombers dropping tin foil strips which produced heavy radar returns.

Elsewhere, between Le Havre and Rouen, Allied planes dropped many hundreds of '*Ruperts*' — dummy paratroopers, half-human sized, which emitted sounds like rifle fire. German units raced off to intercept them. In one area, an entire reserve regiment — some 2,000 men — were committed to chasing the dummies rather than fighting real paratroopers. Finding these dummies — the Germans called them '*explosivpuppen*' — made some German commanders even more convinced that the attack in Normandy now unfolding was nothing more than a diversion.

British radio operators began to cut in on German frequencies, issuing confusing and contradictory orders in German.

After having watched the last of the 101st Airborne take off from their base at Greenham Common with tears in his eyes, Eisenhower had returned to his trailer and now sat there chain-smoking Camels and reading a trashy Western novel. There was no possibility of sleep.

THE GERMAN RESPONSE

On 5 June, the German High Command had received the latest intelligence report.

'*...imminence of invasion is not recognisable,*'

it had said.

The Allied Airborne operations in the early hours of the morning of 6 June caused utter confusion amongst the Germans. By and large, they had not been expecting a paratrooper jump to foreshadow a seaborne invasion and, as more and more telephone lines were cut and German positions knocked out,

no clear picture could be gained of just where the Allies were or what they were doing. Because of the scattered jump, they just seemed to be everywhere.

With stereotypical German efficiency, Colonel Hans von Luck from the 125th Regiment, 21st Panzer Division, sprang into action the moment he heard the first reports of Allied airborne landings at 0130. Within an hour, he had his tanks running their engines, lined up and ready to go. His first plan of attack was to take on the British glider troops at Pegasus Bridge. Unhappily for him, he was refused permission to go. Only the Fuhrer could order panzers into battle — and the Fuhrer was asleep. No — no-one would go and wake him up. He was, after all, the Fuhrer.

General Erich Marcks had just come back from celebrating his birthday in St Lo when his operations room telephoned him to say that there was unusual activity around the Cotentin Peninsula. In a quandary (and not fully sober), Marcks rang General Max Pemsel at the 7th Army HQ in Le Mans. Pemsel duly informed his superior, General Friedrich Dollmann, that, in Pemsel's opinion, the invasion had begun.

Pemsel then phoned Rommel's Chief of Staff General Hans Speidel who in turn called Field Marshal von Rundstedt in Paris. By now, von Rundstedt was also getting calls from the Luftwaffe Commander Field Marshal Hugo Sperrle and Admiral Kranke. There were reports now of huge radar returns out in the Channel, so huge that radar operators suspected their equipment must be malfunctioning. '*A flock of seagulls?*' von Rundstedt suggested unhelpfully.

No one wanted to call Rommel as he was enjoying some well-earned leave with his wife and had an important meeting with the Fuhrer later that day. In a frantic round of phone calls, the German High Command decided that at worst, this was nothing more than Allied diversionary tactics. After all, who would land in Normandy? In this weather? There were even suggestions that local German forces might be overreacting after seeing an Allied bomber crew bale out of a plane. At 0340, General Speidel sent a final dismissive message to Pemsel;

'C in C West does not consider this to be a major operation.'

Requests for further information was confounded when German headquarters
found they could not get through to the local units — and deciding that it was
all much a fuss about nothing most of the senior German officers involved
tucked themselves up in bed..

No one had a clue what was really about to happen
– but by now the invasion armada was loading its
troops onto their landing craft.

'Ships and boats of every nature and size churned the
rough Channel surface, seemingly in a mass so solid one
could have walked from shore to shore.'
Lieutenant Charles Mohrle, P-47 Thunderbolt pilot

'By God, I'll never forget the feeling of power – power about
to be unleashed – that welled up in me as I viewed the long,
endless columns of ships headed towards Normandy.'
Captain Anthony Duke, LST 530

'As God died to make men holy, let us die to make men free.'
(From The Battle Hymn of the Republic, as sung on
board the attack transport USS Bayfield while
crossing the Channel).

UTAH BEACH

'We'll start the war from here.'

Brigadier-General Theodore Roosevelt Junior,
Assistant Division Commander, 4th Infantry

The first American troops hit the beach at 0630. As fate would have it, it was the wrong beach.

Utah beach was the most westerly of the five targeted beaches and because of the orientation of the incoming tide needed to be attacked first. Troops would land at the low point of the tide, when underwater beach obstacles would be most exposed and easier both to avoid and to destroy. Six miles east of St. Mere-Eglise, the beach was some ten miles long and mostly open and

gently sloping. The grey beach sand eventually gave way to tall dunes. Behind the beach was a seawall which ranged from four to twelve feet high, on top of which was the main (but narrow) coast road. The agricultural land on the far side of the road had been deliberately flooded by the Germans. Marshy to begin with, it was now positively treacherous. It could only be safely traversed by four slim causeways, which gave access to the local villages of Audouville, Hebert, St. Martin de Varreville, Pouppeville and St. Germain. If all had gone to plan the previous night, American airborne forces would now have control of all the causeways, allowing the troops on the beaches a swift exit off and inland.

The force tasked with landing on Utah Beach comprised the 4th Infantry Division and the 70th Tank Battalion. They were transported by '*Task Force U*', which had departed from ports in the West Country. The troops bound for Utah had therefore endured both the longest and most gruelling crossing. Before taking to their landing craft, they had already been at sea for some sixty hours. Escorting the Task Force was a formidable assembly of Allied warships, spearheaded by the battleship Nevada and comprising two US Navy cruisers, the Quincy and Tuscaloosa, the RN monitor Erebus and three British cruisers — the Black Prince, Enterprise and Hawkins. A further eight destroyers and a Dutch gunboat completed the force.

The objective of the assault troops was to link up with the paratroopers and then advance on the important port of Cherbourg and prevent the Germans from further reinforcing it.

Facing the Americans were the 91st, 243rd and 709th German Infantry Divisions. Neither the 243rd nor the 709th were highly rated, being comprised of older men, the partially disabled and some 'Ost' soldiers. The 91st was another proposition altogether. Newly arrived in the area, they were considered highly capable and well trained in anti-invasion fighting. It was an unanticipated consequence of the airborne landings that all three divisions were now in a high state of confusion after a night spent trying to deal with pockets of American paratroopers who

seemed to be everywhere. It was also fortunate that the commander of the 91st, Lieutenant-General Wilhelm Falley, had been killed a few hours earlier.

At 0455 on 6 June, the first of a planned twenty four waves of landing craft left the landing ships twelve miles offshore and headed for the beach. The wave consisted of 20 LCVPs, each holding thirty troops, along with four LCTs with thirty-two Sherman tanks on board. The second wave, close in behind was made up of 24 more LCVPs bringing the demolition teams and engineers on shore. Bulldozers and armoured vehicles would come in on the third wave.

Just under an hour later, as they were still heading in, the opening big gun salvos from their naval escorts began, pounding German fortifications on the coastline. The barrage was followed by waves of 300 B-26 Marauder bombers of the 9th US Air Force, hitting the German positions with over four thousand 250lb bombs from under 1,000 feet. Ringing in the crews' *ears was the ferocious briefing given to them by their CO Colonel Wilson — 'let's*

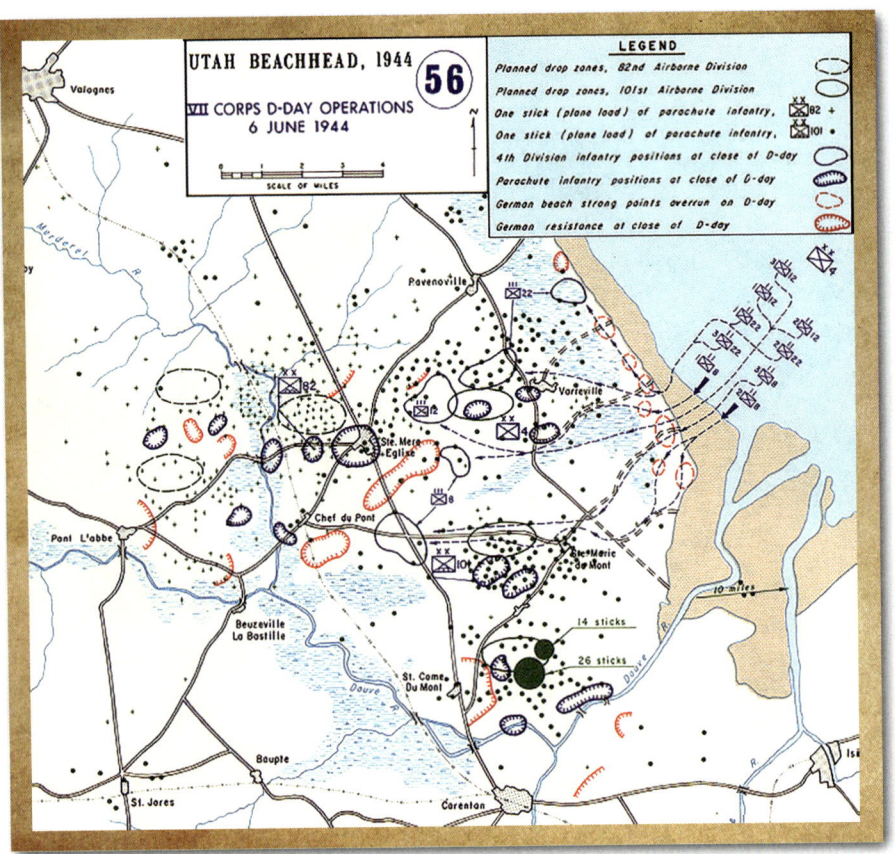

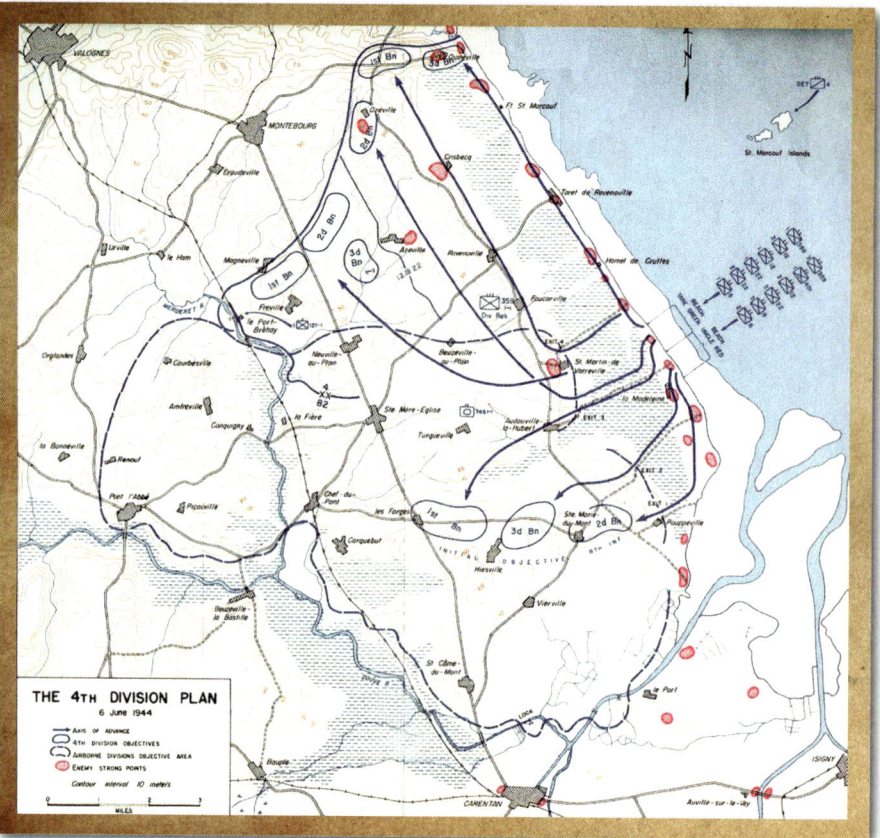

kick the hell out of everything Nazi that's left!' They blazed a ferocious trail of destruction along Utah Beach. Only two bombers were lost.

As the Marauders struck from below cloud level, the rocket-firing LCTRs opened fire simultaneously on the same targets as they powered across the sea. 1,000 2lb rockets rained down in three salvoes on strongpoints, pillboxes and machine gun nests. At Strongpoint W5, all communications were knocked out, so the commander had to resort to using a man on a bicycle to get news of the invasion back to HQ. He never made it. An Allied fighter spotted him pedalling down the road and tore him to pieces with his machine gun.

The beach landings were supposed to be spearheaded by thirty two DD Sherman tanks, scheduled to land at 0630 ahead of any infantry. They would shed their skirts on the beach and then engage the Germans, distracting them and providing covering fire as the infantry made their initial landings. The plan fell apart in the first minutes. Three out of the four boats supposed to control the assault hit new top secret German Oyster mines. In the chaos, the surviving boat gave orders for the DD tanks to be launched just under two miles from shore instead of just over three miles as originally intended. As

the tanks 'swam' for shore, the infantry overtook them. Battling heavy seas and almost completely blinded by the smoke from the bombing and barrage, the men steering the infantry landing craft couldn't tell that the current of the incoming tide was pushing them ever further south — and off course. The result was that the first infantry landing craft hit the beaches unprotected by armour and over a mile south of their intended position, machine gun fire rattling against their landing craft which sounded '*like rocks being chucked at a bathtub.*'. They were lucky. The main strongpoint here had been knocked out by the Marauder attack.

On board the first landing craft to beach was Brigadier-General Theodore Roosevelt Junior, the Assistant Division Commander of the 4th Infantry. Roosevelt was the son of the former president '*Teddy*' Roosevelt and the cousin of the current president. Although in his late fifties and in poor health, Roosevelt had been allowed to land with the first wave to boost morale. '*They'll figure that if a general is going in, it can't be that rough,*' he had joked. Once on land, Roosevelt did his best to sprint across the sand.
Roosevelt spotted almost immediately that his men were in the wrong place, and hastily convened a meeting with Colonel James Van Fleet, Commander of

OPP. PAGE: Operation maps for the Utah Beachhead

BELOW: Landing party members help injured Soldiers to safety on Utah Beach

the 8th Regiment, in a convenient foxhole. As he saw it, there were two choices. The landing forces could either fight their way over a mile north along the beach to the designated landing spot at Les Dunes de Varreville , or else force their way inland from here and call in all successive waves on their new position. To Roosevelt, the decision wasn't difficult. By a stroke of luck, the position where they had landed was poorly defended by comparison with their original landing zone, which had at its heart two large German strongpoints bristling with guns. As the first troops surged up the beach around him, they were so surprised and delighted by the lack of opposition that they started cheering and waving their carbines in the air. 'We'll start the war from here,' he announced, emerging from the shell hole to wave his walking stick forward at the troops already streaming past him. Roosevelt was to win the Medal of Honor for his actions on D-Day — only to die of a heart attack some five weeks later,.

A second wave of troops had landed just five minutes behind the first along with engineers and demolition teams to tackle the beach obstacles. At 0645, a third wave brought in sixteen regular Sherman tanks and a number of bulldozers.

The German opposition along the stretch of beach was not only relatively weak: It was also collectively in shock after being on the receiving end of almost two hours of combined big gun salvoes, waves of rockets and bombing. Strongpoints W2 and W5 had both had their 88mm artillery guns knocked out and were firing back with whatever they could scrape together.

As the amphibious DD tanks finally made their way on shore some fifteen minutes later — twenty-eight out of the initial thirty-two — the Germans were also stunned by the sight of swimming tanks, something no-one had ever warned them about. Hastily, the commander of the St. Marie du Pont strongpoint tried to deploy their own secret weapon against the DDs — miniature remote controlled 'Goliath' suicide tanks, each packed with 224lb of high explosive. The intent was to drive them up against an Allied tank

OPP. PAGE: U.S. troops disembarking on Utah Beach, 6 June 1944. The LCVP in the foreground was assigned to the U.S. Navy attack transport USS Joseph T. Dickman, which had sailed from England on 5 June and landed her troops without a mishap, and steamed to Portland with casualties in the afternoon of 6 June 1944

BELOW L–R: US soldiers land on Utah Beach. On the beach, carcasses of destroyed vehicles lie scattered; Carrying full equipment, American assault troops move onto Utah Beach on the northern coast of France; U.S. Soldiers of the 8th Infantry Regiment, 4th Infantry Division, move out over the seawall on Utah Beach after coming ashore. Other troops are resting behind the concrete wall

and then detonate them. It was quickly discovered that their remote control mechanism had been damaged in the bombardment, however, and they stubbornly refused to work. The strongpoint opened up on the Americans with machine guns and mortars instead, only to receive a blistering big gun salvo from the warships in reply. Elsewhere, the Americans met only light resistance, encountering shell-shocked German defenders almost too willing to surrender at the first opportunity.

As more waves of landing craft swept in, news of the invasion began to reach German gun emplacements further back from the beach and they opened up, but with little accuracy as there were no adequate forward observers. When the shelling did start to become more accurate, it was quickly discovered that the Germans were using the barrage balloons aloft over Allied vessels as markers, and these were swiftly cut adrift and left to float away. They were

engaged in turn by the warships, the USS Nevada replying so ferociously that the paint peeled off her gun barrels. As the shells came in, US Navy Seabees worked frantically to clear beach obstacles to pave the way for more and more armour and transport vehicles to beach. Within the first hour after landing, they had succeeded in clearing eight fifty-yard holes in the obstacles to allow multiple corridors off the beach and onto the coastal road on the sea wall. Despite their best efforts, a potentially threatening 'traffic jam' began to build up as more and more men and vehicles arrived.

While the fighting was relatively light, US troops storming off the beaches along the causeways and into the land beyond encountered much more danger from concealed minefields, and these caused the majority of casualties on Utah that day. Mines also knocked out a number of tanks. Particularly dreaded by the infantry was the S-Mine, colloquially called the 'Bouncing Betty'. Once triggered, the mine would be projected up out of the ground to groin height — and would then explode.

Just after 1100, advanced scouts from heading inland off the beach met up with General Taylor and men of the 101st Airborne at Pouppeville. After an unfortunate but brief friendly fire incident, the beach troops and the 101st then joined forces to take St. Marie du Mont.

While the accidental landing site had been a blessing in terms of low casualties, it had left the 12th Infantry Regiment particularly badly out of position. One of their first tasks had been to secure St. Martin de Varreville. That now lay well to the north, and moving off on the coast road was difficult

because of the sheer weight of men, tanks, lorries and jeeps using it. Exit 2 was the only route available. Frustrated, Colonel Russell Reeder, commander of the 12th, ordered his men to manoeuvre through the flooded fields to reach their target, rather than wait for the road congestion to ease up. Reeder had been briefed that the flooded areas were only around eighteen inches deep. The truth was the water was more than waist high and — should a soldier step into a concealed ditch beneath the surface, he would suddenly be completely submerged and dragged down by the weight of his equipment. The GIs struggled on across the flooded terrain for over a mile, swimmers keeping a careful eye on non-swimmers and using ropes to span the hidden ditches once found. Their progress was made even harder by sporadic sniper fire. Once back on dry land, the GIs met up with elements of the 82nd Airborne who had taken St. Martin de Varreville.

The traffic jam on Utah did not clear until mid-afternoon, and as troops surged inland, they were further reinforced by glider units.

The taking of Utah Beach was one of the great successes of D-Day. In just fifteen hours, the Americans successfully landed over 23,000 troops and 1,700 vehicles of all descriptions. Although the forces at Utah only succeeded in capturing about half the territory intended on Day One and German resistance locally was far from crushed, by evening, lead elements of the 4th Infantry were a good eight miles inland and the beachhead was considered secure. The paratroopers fighting to hold St. Mère-Eglise would not be properly relieved for several days although friendly forces were now just a mile outside of town. Cherbourg itself would finally fall on 26 June. Casualties were also far, far lighter than expected. The 12th Regiment lost sixty-nine men killed or wounded and between them, the 8th and 22nd regiments saw just twelve fatalities, along with a further 106 wounded. It was the combat engineering units who suffered the highest casualties along with the tankers and ships crews. Approximately 700 died. One of the eight destroyers, the USS Corry, was also lost, either to a mine or to return fire from coastal batteries. Although the ship tore in two before sinking, losses from her crew were mercifully light.

Just along the coast however, things were very different...

OMAHA BEACH

'Two kinds of people are staying on this beach, the dead and those who are going to die. Now let's get the hell out of here!'

Colonel George Taylor, 16th RCT Commander

' They're murdering us here. Let's move inland and get murdered..'

Colonel Charles Canham, Commander, 116th Infantry Regiment

It was on 'Bloody Omaha' Beach that things started to wrong almost from the beginning – and proceeded to get very much worse.

There had been concerns about the difficulties of storming Omaha Beach before the invasion got underway. General Bradley had been warned that Omaha was 'formidable'. And so it was. The target beaches of Omaha spread for some six miles from the north-west on the Allies' right flank to the south east on the left, extending from Vierville-sur-Mer to Colville-sur-Mer. The area chosen formed a natural crescent — just perfect for concentrating fire on the beaches. The beaches themselves transformed from sand to shingle as they reached a low beach wall. Beyond the wall was marshy grassland and then formidable sandy bluffs rising up to 150 feet above the beach area.

These '*heights*' could only be reached by ascending five steep ravines. The Germans had each and every one heavily fortified. To the northwest, the beach ended hard up against huge cliffs. The beach approach itself was naturally treacherous, with hidden sandbars and vicious currents, but to add to the threat on approach the Germans had planted three distinct layers of obstacles.

RIGHT: Operational maps for the assault on Omaha Beach

OPP. PAGE: Troops in an LCVP landing craft approaching "Omaha" Beach on "D-Day", 6 June 1944

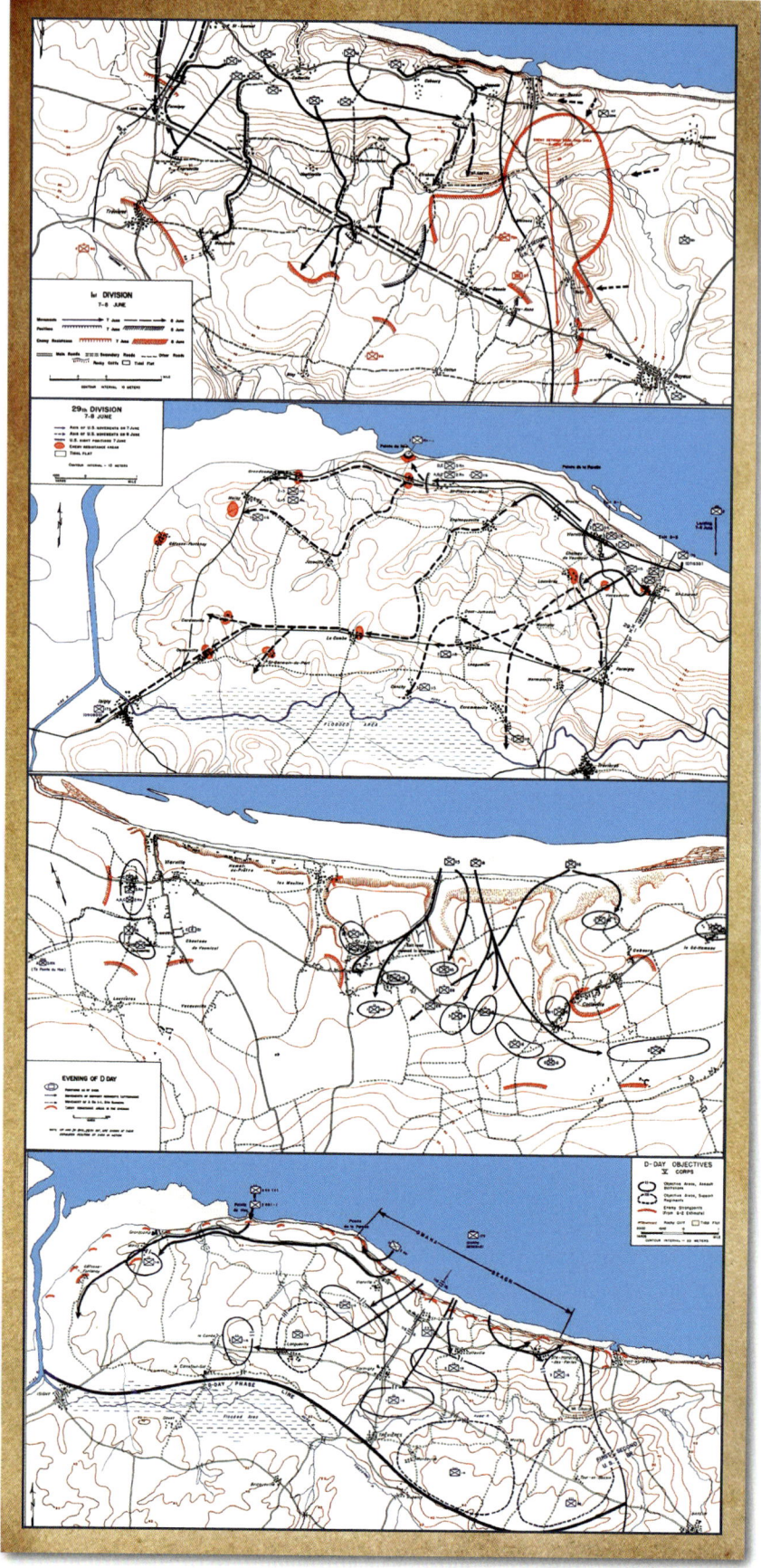

First there were fierce iron girder structures some ten feet high off the sand bristling with Teller mines. Then came a double row of jutting wooden poles sunk deep onto the sand and again covered with mines. Finally came rows of '*Hedgehogs*', constructions of angled steel designed to tear holes in landing craft. There were also hidden mines and booby-traps, especially concentrated just beyond the sea wall and swathed in dense barbed wire coils.

Beyond, the Germans had built concrete strongpoints to guard the ravine exits.

They would typically comprise a large artillery gun, a 50mm cannon and ten Spandau machine guns operated by a supporting infantry platoon. Facing out to sea there were a further eight major concrete bunkers mostly boasting 88mm guns, as well as sixty emplacements for light artillery, and over fifty pill boxes containing either artillery pieces or anti-tank guns. Between the bunkers and the pillboxes stretched zig-zagging infantry trenches, defended by wire and bristling with machine guns. Behind this line of defences, just to the rear there were forty rocket and mortar pits. One strongpoint even had automatic flamethrowers.

OPP. PAGE: Digitally colorized image of '*Into the Jaws of Death*', a photograph by Robert F Sargent of the United States Army First Infantry Division disembarking from an LCVP onto Omaha Beach during the Normandy Landings, June 6, 1944

BELOW L–R: German turret at Omaha Beach, June 1944; Approaching Omaha; The build-up of Omaha Beach. soldiers and equipment moving inland

To add to the problems facing the Americans, the area had recently been reinforced by elements of the hardened German 352nd fresh from the Eastern Front, replacing some of the Ost troops the Americans had been expecting to fight. In total there were some 800 Germans of the 352nd defending the beach positions — and this didn't include Maisy — a massive German gun battery with six 155mm guns up on the sheer cliffs at Pointe du Hoc which enjoyed a perfect field of fire down on to the beach and which was targeted to be taken out in a separate operation by 2nd Battalion, US Army Rangers.

The American forces entrusted with taking Omaha beach were of varying quality. The area to the west was given to the 29th Infantry Division, which consisted very heavily of troops who had never seen battle while taking the eastern sector fell to the more experienced 1st Infantry Division — the famous '*Big Red One*'. The objective assigned to the American forces was to secure both the beaches and the land behind to a depth of five miles between Port-en-Bessin and the Vire River, join up with the British next door on Gold Beach and link up with their fellow Americans coming off Utah Beach. Omaha then,

rather than having specific cities or communications routes as its objective, was essentially meant to serve as a bridge between Utah and Gold beaches.

German observers had spotted the naval task force offshore at around 0500 and opened fire with coastal artillery. The destroyer USS Emmons, together with the battleship Arkansas and the Free French cruiser Georges Leygues were already duelling with the German batteries when the official bombardment, comprising some 2,000 shells, commenced at 0550. Fifteen minutes later, over three hundred USAAF B-17 Flying Fortresses and B-24 Liberators rolled in to bomb thirteen targets on the shore and behind the immediate defences. They dropped 13,000 bombs — and missed. The cloud cover was low and too thick for accurate aiming and some bombs fell as much as three miles off target. The bombardment over, the Germans prepared to fight, their defensive positions largely untouched.

At 0540, thirty-two Sherman DD tanks from the 741st Tank Battalion launched 5,000 yards out from the shore. They slipped straight into waves as high as six feet tall and were swamped and battered from the moment they entered the sea. Flotation skirts began to rip. Struts snapped and sea water slopped into the engines. They were simply overwhelmed. Twenty-seven sank to the bottom, sometimes with their crews sealed and trapped inside, fighting to get out. Over thirty tankers died, the rest, struggled for their lives in the water as landing craft packed with infantrymen swept passed. (Only five of the tanks eventually made it to shore — and three of them were destroyed in minutes by ferocious anti-tank fire from the shore fortifications.) Spotting the disaster unfolding, the American officer responsible for releasing the DD tanks of the

OPP. PAGE: Crossed rifles in the sand are a comrade's tribute to this American soldier who sprang ashore from a landing barge and died at the barricades

BELOW L-R: American assault troops of the 3d Battalion, 16th Infantry Regiment, 1st U.S. Infantry Division, who stormed Omaha Beach; A medic of the 3d Bn., 16th Inf. Regt., 1st U.S. Inf. Div., moves along a narrow strip of Omaha Beach administering first aid to men wounded in the landing; Large group of American assault troops of the 3d Battalion, 16th Infantry Regiment, 1st U.S. Infantry Division, having gained the comparative safety offered by the chalk cliff at their backs, takes a "breather" before moving inland

743rd thought better of it and decided to take the Shermans in by boat rather than letting them swim ashore under their own power.

As the first wave came in at 0635, fire was directed onto the German defences by thirty-six M7 Priest howitzers and thirty-four tanks on board their inbound LCTs, together with rocket salvos from craft designated as rocket launchers riding in together, line abreast. 14,000 rockets fizzed and shrieked their way over the Higgins Boats towards the beach defences. All missed, and fell short into the sea…

In came the first waves of American infantry — 1,450 men in thirty-six wildly tipping and bucking landing craft from the 116th of the 29th and the 16th of the 1st — directly into a furious hail of everything the Germans could throw at them. Over ten landing craft were destroyed before they could even lower their ramps. There were few survivors. A direct artillery hit would throw corpses sixty feet into the air. Other soldiers pitched into the freezing water

simply sank to the bottom, weighed down by their equipment. Daunted by the fire, some craft swerved wildly and became lodged on sandbars, their men trapped out at sea. Other landing craft lowered their ramps too soon, and soldiers charged out only to find themselves in water 12-15 foot deep. They sank too, desperately trying to free themselves from the weight of their packs. Those craft which did make it to the beach opened their ramps and found themselves the perfect targets for German Spandau machine gunners, with thirty men all packed together and now completely exposed to fire as they tried to run from the craft. Whole platoons were mown down in a matter of seconds, men choosing to vault over the sides into deep water rather than face the direct fire concentrated on the ramps. . German artillery and mortars joined in with the machine guns. To many of the troops coming in, it felt like suicide to attempt to run the beach.

Those who did make into onto the sands huddled behind beach obstacles — often without their guns or equipment — and tried to get their bearings. Most of the landing craft had been swept to the east by the tide by over half a mile and they could not identify their objectives. Beside them, exhausted survivors from landing craft sunk further out to sea struggled up onto the sands and were shot dead — or simply collapsed with exhaustion and were drowned by the incoming tide. In just five bloody minutes, 90% of the initial assault troops were pinned down, dead or wounded.

Fifty-eight tanks of the 743rd finally came in to offer some support. Unfortunately A Company came in right in a straight line with the heavily defended Vieville ravine. In a matter of just minutes, half of its DD Tanks were

OPP. PAGE: Landing ships putting cargo ashore on Omaha Beach, at low tide during the first days of the operation

knocked out and all but one of its officers were dead. B and C companies landing elsewhere fared better, although they too started taking losses from the moment they landed. The survivors would prove more and more valuable as the morning wore on, having the firepower to crack the German defences. However, co-ordinating with the requirements of infantry proved almost impossible.

As the first wave troops struggled to survive at the water's edge, more craft came in behind them. This time they carried 270 combat engineers, but the engineers took the same hammering as the first assault troops. Many carried TNT on their bodies to blow up the beach obstacles and — if hit by a single unfortunate bullet round — would just explode and leave next to nothing behind. Within minutes, the engineers realised they had lost over 60% of their equipment and were scattered up and down the beach. To reach German mines planted on top of the obstacles, one engineer had to stand on another's shoulders — making them perfect and obvious targets for snipers. Only five teams of the sixteen landed ever made it to their designated objectives. Only three bulldozers made it to shore, the other thirteen being lost at sea or hit and blown up by enemy fire on the shoreline. Engineers also found the troops huddled behind the beach obstacles distinctly unwilling to leave their shelter so that the engineers could begin demolition. The effect was to make clearing exits off the beach a painfully slow business, jamming up following waves and concentrating them into small areas which the Germans could then saturate with fire.

Those who attempted the beach run — some 500 yards over totally exposed ground — were cut to pieces by meticulously planned German crossfire, but some made it to the protection of a small shale bank and sea wall. Here, at least partly sheltered from the bullets, they halted. Others on other areas of the beach were not so fortunate. All they had for shelter were loose sand dunes — but at least smoke from the grass fires burning atop the dunes provided some sort of cover. Directly ahead was a minefield choked with coils of barbed wire. If they could cross that, they would still have to assault uphill against the fortified German positions on the bluff. Behind them, more and more men in the second wave were landing and taking heavy losses before the survivors joined them pressed against the shale bank, as trapped as the first wave. On board an LCA on the second wave was an American photographer for Life Magazine, Robert Capa. Plunged headlong into the

carnage, he took 111 photos of the battle as it unfolded, often whilst under fire. He managed to get his precious rolls of film back to safety — and then found that a hapless 16-year-old lab assistant had accidentally exposed almost all the reels. Only eleven of his photographs of Omaha on D-Day survived.

All communication with the ships off shore had been lost, but the US Navy could see what was happening anyway. Destroyers started closing towards the shallows and picking their own targets, coming in so close (less than 1,000 yards) that German bullets were ricocheting off their hulls. They lowered their guns and pumped fire directly into the German fortifications on the bluff.

From the entire first wave, only one infantry company had been able to fight and attack as a cohesive unit. All the rest had been scattered and mixed together in the thick clumps of Khaki now squatting in the dunes or huddled against the sea wall. Seeing the carnage as they came in, many landing craft crews had elected to drop their men where defensive fire seemed less intense, but this had only succeeded in jumbling up the different companies involved. Surviving officers to give instructions were few and far between and — as they led from the front as an example to their men — those few that had made it off the beach began to be killed off too. Snipers made them a priority.

'Get these men the hell off this beach! Go kill some goddamned Krauts!

Colonel Charles D. 'Old Hatchetface' Canham, CO, 116th Infantry Regiment

By 0830, landings were started to be suspended, resulting in a traffic jam of ships out at sea. By 0900 there were 5,000 men fighting to stay alive on the beaches.

The second wave brought in headquarters units and some seriously high ranking officers who desperately tried to install order into the chaos. Gradually small groups began to form and to take the initiative. The troops huddled in shelter realised that if they didn't advance they would surely be killed. Bangalore torpedoes now appeared as if from nowhere. Men started to blow holes in the wire and the minefield and struggle forward. Many were killed,

LEFT: General Omar Bradley

RIGHT: General Dietrich Kraiss

pinned on the wire and shot or blown up by undetected mines, but enough made it through to begin assembling at the base of the bluff.

Sometime after 0900 elements of the 16th Infantry were successful in storming one of the five ravines to the west and made it to the top of the bluff. They began to work their way along, storming German slit trenches and taking out pillboxes and gun batteries one by one, Taking part in the action, Private Ray Moon looked back down and later recalled;

'The beach was a shooting gallery for machine gunners. The scene below reminded me of the Chicago stockyard cattle pens and its slaughter house…'

Germans started to surrender — only to be machine gunned by other German troopers offended by their cowardice. Men of the 116th Infantry also progressed up the bluff at roughly the same time under the direction of General Norman '*Dutch*' Cota and likewise started taking out the German coast positions before moving away off the beach to take Vierville. Here they met other GIs who had also made it off the beach and drew up plans to attack the surviving German beach positions from the rear and free up more of the exit routes. The GIs under Cota became known as '*Cota*'s *Bastard Brigade.*'

Shortly after 1000 the decision had been taken by commanders offshore to throw in the reserves and the 115th Infantry from the 29th duly landed at 1045. They moved through one of the four breeches now opened up and over the bluff and attacked St Laurent. The situation on Omaha had now improved markedly, but this news had not reached General Bradley, on board the USS Augusta who seriously considered abandoning Omaha altogether and landing his men on the British Gold Beach instead. It was also agreed to bomb Omaha Beach, erroneously believing that it was still held by the Germans. Thankfully, this never came to pass. Instead, by 1230 18,772 GIs were ashore.

In a supreme irony, the local German commander, General Dietrich Kraiss of the 352nd, also believed that he had succeeded in stopping the Americans cold on Omaha, receiving erroneous reports of a resounding German victory as late as 1335. Based on this, he decided to commit his reserves to fighting the British coming ashore instead at Gold. (A significant part of this reserve — '*Kampfgruppe Meyer*' — who had been out chasing '*Ruperts*' the night before — were slaughtered later that day). The ideal opportunity for the Germans to launch an effective counterattack against the battered and precariously positioned Americans was therefore missed. By the end of the day, having obtained a clearer picture of events, General Kraiss would be pleading for reinforcements, only to be told that none were available.

Sporadic fighting continued for the rest of the day. Colleville was lost and won back from the Germans several times. It was also hit by friendly fire from naval warships, killing sixty-four GIs. St Laurent was surrounded but not taken, and the German garrison there held out until the next day. By and large, the troops having fought through a truly traumatic ordeal felt entitled now to rest up and recuperate — and their commanding officers thought it wise not to disagree. It was not until 1720 hours that signals were sent that it was now safe enough to bring more vehicles ashore. On the beach, bodies were reported as being stacked '*like lumber.*'

At the end of D-Day, the American forces on Omaha had suffered 3,000 casualties (one thousand fatalities) as well as over 50 tanks and had barely progressed inland, but they did hold a beach area 10,000 yards wide by 3,000 deep and 34,000 men were now ashore. It was reported that men on the beach would find it hard to eat for several days after, because of the clinging smell of burned human flesh. The beach was still sporadically under fire from artillery and a number of German strongpoints remained that were still fighting, albeit surrounded now. Engineers had opened thirteen separate gaps to get men and machines safely off the beach. Support artillery and more and more men, materials and vehicles were pouring ashore to solidify their hold with every incoming wave of ships, but only 100 tons of the planned 2,400 tons of supplies had been successfully landed and there were shortages of everything from food to bullets.

POINTE DU HOC

'No soldier in my command has ever been wished a more difficult task than that which befell the thirty-four-year-old Commander of this Provisional Ranger Force.'

General Bradley, talking of Rangers leader Lieutenant Colonel James Earl Rudder.

'Three old women with brooms could keep the Rangers from climbing that cliff,'

Unnamed US Intelligent Officer before the mission

D-Day's toughest mission was assigned to the elite American Rangers – the force others referred to as The Suicide Squad.

Situated on the Pointe du Hoc at the top of sheer one hundred foot high cliffs to

the Allies' far right and just outside the area of Omaha Beach, the gun battery codenamed Maisey had been designated as the most dangerous defensive position in the entire American sector. It comprised six WWI vintage French 155mm guns, all with perfect sight of both the Omaha and Utah invasion beaches. Four were in reinforced concrete casemates and the remaining two were in the process of being given protection. The guns were guarded by a garrison of 210 German soldiers and artillerymen. The soldiers were expected to be low grade Ost troops but just a week before D-Day they had been replaced by far more capable Germans from the 352nd Infantry Division.

The RAF bombed it. USAAF bombed it. On the morning of 6 June, the USS Texas blitzed it with fourteen inch shells. In total it was hit within just a few hours by the high explosive power of the Hiroshima bomb — and it survived intact. It would have be taken the hard way — by infantry assault.

The tasks of scaling the formidable 100 foot cliffs and closing with the battery had been assigned to the two hundred and twenty five men of the 2nd Battalion of the US Army Rangers under the command of Lieutenant Colonel James Earl Rudder. *'Rudders' Rangers'* as they were known had spent much of the year training with British Commandos, honing their climbing skills first in

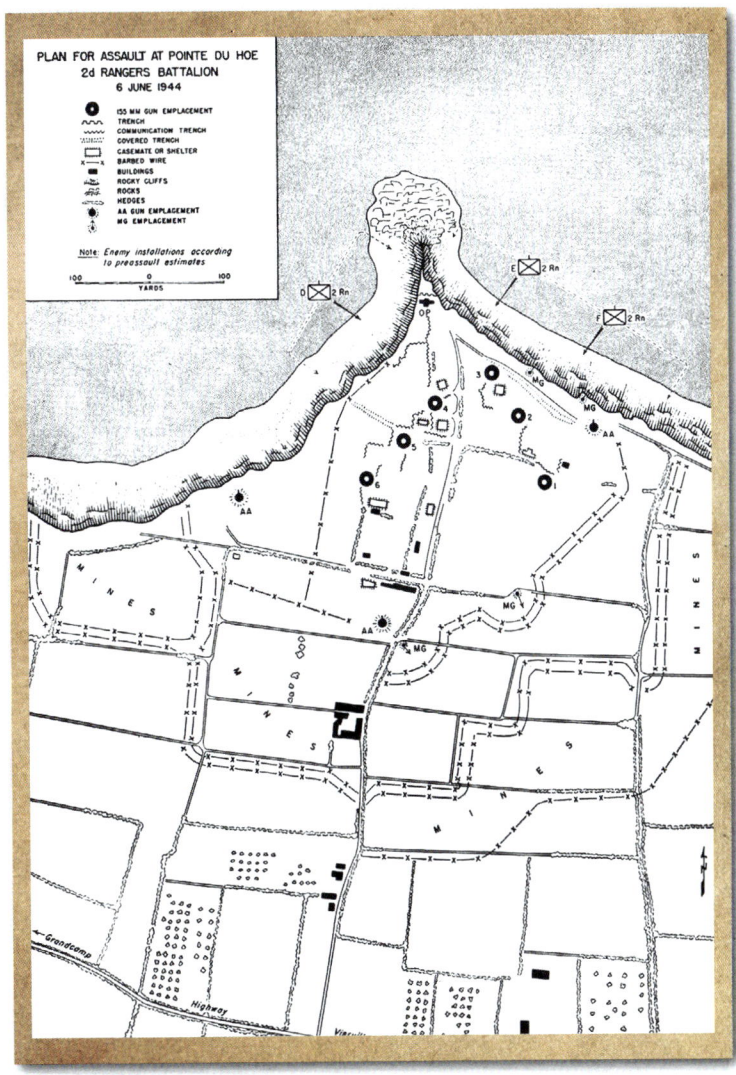

PLAN FOR ASSAULT AT POINTE DU HOE
2d RANGERS BATTALION
6 JUNE 1944

● 155 MM GUN EMPLACEMENT
∧∧∧ TRENCH
COMMUNICATION TRENCH
COVERED TRENCH
CASEMATE OR SHELTER
×—× BARBED WIRE
■ BUILDINGS
ROCKY CLIFFS
ROCKS
HEDGES
AA GUN EMPLACEMENT
MG EMPLACEMENT

Note: Enemy installations according to preassault estimates

100   0   100
YARDS

OPP. PAGE: Observation bunker of Pointe du Hoc

LEFT: Operational map of Pointe du Hoc

BELOW L-R: U.S. Army Rangers resting in the vicinity of Pointe du Hoc; Photo taken on Day 2, after relief forces reached the Rangers at Point du Hoc; American soldiers at Pointe du Hoc

Scotland and then on the Isle of Wight and in Dorset. To help them in their task they brought in specialised equipment including ten LCAs designed to fire lines and ladders with grappling hooks, propelled by rockets up and over the cliff. Hand-held rocket line launchers were also carried along with special lightweight ladders. Finally, they also had four DUKW amphibious vehicles each with a 100-foot ladder provided courtesy of the London Fire Brigade.

The seas were cruel as the Rangers got moving twelve miles out from shore at 0445. One of the boats carrying invaluable supplies capsized and sank, killing almost everyone on board. A second supply boat was forced to jettison a full half of its equipment just to stay afloat. One of the landing craft carrying the Rangers then sank too and only a frantic rescue mission saved twenty-two of the men on board. As the remaining LCAs came in, the men on board were forced to frantically bail sea water out of the craft with their helmets to stop them sinking too. And then they discovered they were going the wrong way.

In the half-light of morning, Pointe et Raz de la Percee had been mistaken for Pointe du Hoc and the remaining Ranger force were now going hell for leather for the wrong headland. Fortunately the mistake was realised and the Ranger force

LEFT: Bombing of Pointe du Hoc by Ninth Air Force bombers

changed course — but it made them thirty-four minutes late in landing. They came in at 0704 instead of 0630 — which meant they would now be landing under the very noses of the Germans in broad daylight. They were shot at constantly as they diverted a mile and a half along the coastline. Only four of the ten LCAs which had set out made it to shore. The rest floundered and sank but most of the Rangers on board survived to struggle through the shallows and rejoin their unit.

The Rangers took immediate fire from the clifftop with Germans leaning over the edge, shooting at them or simply dropping down hand grenades. Huddling for protection against the base of the cliff on a tiny strip of beach, the Rangers began to fire off their personal grappling line rockets — only to discover that they didn't work properly due to being drenched with sea water on the way in. Lines fell short, grappling hooks could not find purchase in the grass atop the cliff and the soaked ropes were hard to grip and then climb. Above them, German soldiers took their bayonets and started cutting those lines that had reached the height, sending several Rangers plunging to their deaths. To provide some support, the battleship USS Texas and destroyers USS Satterlee and HMS Talybont furiously bombarded the Germans on the clifftop, turning the whole elevated area into a heavily cratered wasteland resembling the lunar surface.

The surviving amphibious vehicles with their Fire Brigade ladders had great difficulty raising them to full height because of the cliff's overhang but at least one became fully extended. A Ranger sergeant scaled it and stood at the top, swaying widely as he sprayed the German defenders with bullets from his Tommy Gun.

Slowly but surely more and more Rangers made it up the cliff and the Germans began to fall back. Eventually a naval fire control party joined them and began to direct naval salvos from the Satterlee and McCook onto smaller German gun positions with almost unerring accuracy. Whole gun emplacements were blown off the top of the cliff by the force of the explosions. Having gained control of the cliffs, the surviving Rangers then moved inland towards Maisey itself. They took heavy casualties from a German counter-attack but succeeded in driving it back.

By 0830 the first Rangers had reached Maisey. It was empty. The big guns had all gone. Initially there was utter confusion amongst the completely exhausted Rangers. The Germans had obviously moved them several days ago — but to where? And could they still be fired? A frantic search began. It transpired that

Maisey's big guns were only 200 yards away, set up in new, well camouflaged positions in an orchard — but the gun crews were nowhere to be seen. Rangers set about sabotaging and spiking them, dropping thermite grenades down their barrels. Off went the signal — 'Praise the Lord' meaning they had succeeded.

Maisey's guns were out of action — but now the Rangers had to survive with their backs to a sheer drop into the sea. They were expecting eight more companies of Rangers to join them off Omaha Beach by noon as reinforcements. The promised reinforcements would not reach them until D-Day +2. German counter attacks came in. Each was beaten off in fierce fighting. The Rangers were constantly shot at by a distant mg post until a naval round blew the entire German edifice into the sea. The Rangers kept calling in fire support until their fire control party was wiped out. After that, they communicated with the big ships via an old Aldis lamp.

By 2100 hours the Rangers were still fighting to survive, keeping fresh German reserves at bay. They too had received some reinforcements — three very lost American paratroopers from the 101st Airborne and just twenty-three men from the 5th Rangers who had become separated from their main force on Omaha and had fought their way to Pointe du Hoc instead. By now though the Rangers had suffered a full 1/3rd casualties killed or wounded and were short of everything from ammunition to food and water.

Come night, the Germans launched three successive counter attacks, the last of which succeeded and forced the Americans to retreat to new and narrow defensive positions. Here they would spend the night.

Morning on D-Day+1 saw the Rangers on Ponte du Hoc completely out of food and down to just one hundred men capable of fighting. An attempt to evacuate the wounded failed when a rescue boat off the USS Harding was hit. A second boat brought in food, communications equipment and bullets — and incredibly, the Rangers decided to fight on instead of being evacuated. With full stomachs and magazines and an ability to call in navy fire support, they succeeded in driving the local German forces back all the way south of the N13 road. Although some concealed German guns remained active in the area until D-Day +3, at 1130 on D-Day+2, fighting had finally eased up enough for the Stars and Stripes to be raised over Pointe du Hoc by Rudder's Rangers. By now, they had suffered seventy-seven killed and 152 wounded.

GOLD BEACH

'Once you stop on the beach, you are never going to get up again.'

Major George Young, 6th Battalion, the Green Howards

Gold was at the centre of the five D-Day beaches, stretching some ten miles from Port-en-Bessin in the west to La Rivière in the east. To the west lay Omaha and the Americans, to the east Juno and the Canadians. German strength amounted to some 2,000 men mostly from the 352nd and 716th Infantry Divisions. Beach forces were essentially concentrated in two places — La Riviere to the east of Gold Beach and at Le Hamel almost central along the beachfront. Both strongpoints were in existing French buildings — now heavily reinforced and fortified, rather than having been especially designed and constructed. As a result, both were vulnerable to supporting naval salvos or aerial bombardment. At the western end of Gold lay particularly uninviting and steep cliffs. This effectively confined the practical landing area to the beaches between La Riviere and Le Hamel.

Ranged against the German defenders were the British 231st Infantry Brigade to the west and the 69th Infantry Brigade to the east on their left. Their objectives were ambitious. The 231st had to take and hold Le Hamel, then move west to seize the resort town of Arromanches. 47 Commando would capture the small port of Port-en-Bessin and meet up with the American forces advancing off Omaha Beach. To the East, the 69th was to wrest control of La Riviere and eventually link up with the Canadians from Juno. The 56th

Infantry Brigade would arrive in the second wave near Le Hamel to sweep south, cutting the N13 road and taking Bayeux, which lay six miles south west of the coast. At La Riviere, the 151st Infantry Brigade, was tasked with capturing the Caen road and railway and establish good defensive positions on high ground between the rivers Aure and Seulles.

The action began with an intensive Allied air bombardment from medium and heavy bombers, followed by salvos of naval gunfire from some eighteen ships, mainly cruisers and destroyers. As the big naval guns opened up, the first wave of assault troops were already scrambling into their LCAs. First off were the Royal Engineers and underwater demolition teams to tackle anticipated beach obstacles and mines.

It was quickly discovered that the gun emplacements atop the cliffs near Longues-sur-Mer had not been knocked out by the bombardment. They opened fire shortly after dawn, forcing the HQ ship for Gold to move away to safety

OPP. PAGE: Men of 6th Battalion, the Green Howards, in an assault landing craft during Exercise '*Fabius*', 5 May 1944

BELOW L-R: A Cromwell Mk IV tank of 7th Armoured Division, with infantry aboard, comes ashore from an LST on Gold beach; Commandos of the 50th (Northumbrian) Infantry Division of the British Army coming ashore from Landing Craft Infantry at Gold Beach; Commandos of 47 (RM) Commando coming ashore from LCAs on Green beach

OPP. PAGE: The U.S. Coast Guard manned USS LST-21 unloads British Army tanks and trucks onto a "Rhino" barge during the early hours of the invasion on Gold Beach

BELOW: Operational map of Gold Beach

and also threatening the US Navy battleship Arkansas, which was then lending support to the troops on next door Omaha Beach. The Royal Navy cruiser HMS Ajax, supported by the Argonaut, moved in to intercede, and began a ferocious duel with the shore batteries. As its six inch shells slammed into the reinforced concrete of the gun posts, the nerves of the German gunners soon collapsed in two of the posts and they fled. The third post kept on firing its 155mm gun until a lucky shell from the Ajax passed right through the open slit of the post, exploding and killing everyone inside at around 0700 hrs.

Sherman tanks on board LCT's began firing at the shoreline from just over seven miles out and the self-propelled guns and 25-pounders in the craft behind them were soon joining in, firing ragged salvos with each field piece

shooting off an average of three shells a minute. Rocket craft supported the bombardment from closer in shore. At 400 yards, the leading LCAs fired a volley of 24 spigot bombs, each containing 30lb of high explosives in an attempt to clear one thirty-six foot wide gap through the beach obstacles for the tanks and '*Funnies*' to get through and engage the enemy at close range. Because of rough seas, the thirty-eight DD Tanks were not released until very close to the shore and — in some cases — were even delivered directly onto the beaches for their own safety. As the LCTs came in, they suffered significant damage from mines. At least twenty were hit.

Resistance to the first assault troops hitting the beach was patchy. In places, the beach was defended by Russian '*Ost*' soldiers who were quite eager to surrender given an opportunity, but resistance remained strong in other places.

The German strongpoint in Le Hamel, enjoying mortar support from rear units, managed to lay down such fierce machine gun and mortar fire on the first wave (comprising the 1st Dorsetshires and 1st Hampshires) that they were largely pinned on the beach and watched as the '*Funnies*' ahead of them went to work

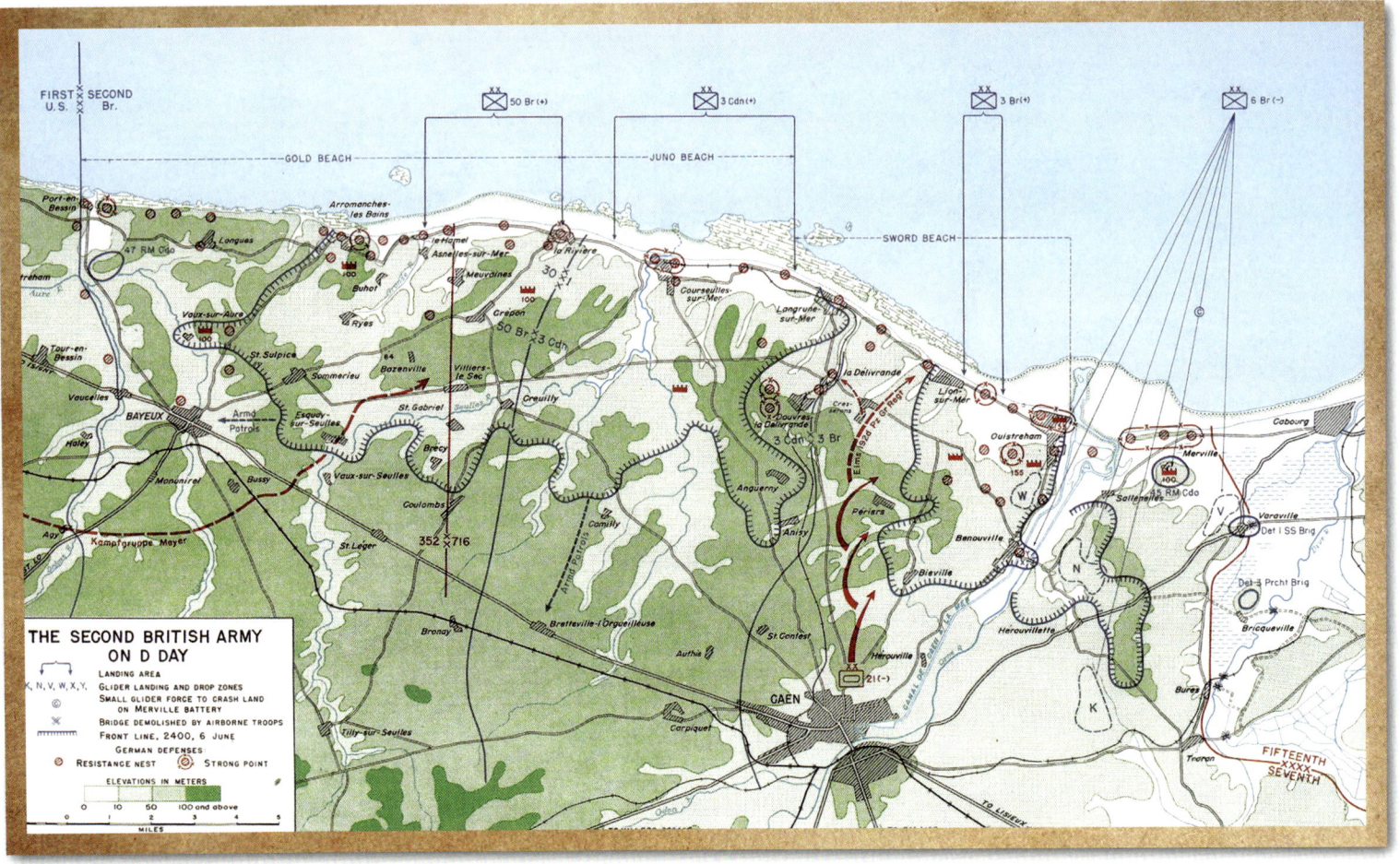

flailing through minefields until they too were knocked out. The surviving crews joined the infantry huddled in hastily dug foxholes or up against the seawall. Given the strength of resistance the first wave had met, the second wave was directed to land well to either side of them and keep clear. The assault troops landed at 0725 but it was well over half an hour later that the first tank support arrived to help them, by which time their CO and many other officers had become casualties. When the tanks finally came in, a number found themselves immediately bogged down in the particularly soft sand or else were hit and knocked out right on the shoreline by determined enemy resistance. Fire from the Le Hamel strongpoint proved so difficult to subdue that the Hampshires decided to flank it in both directions, preferring to fight their way inland through other German fortifications and obstacles. After another assault on the heart of Le Hamel failed, it was decided only to attack the strongpoint from the rear. An 88mm gun emplacement managed to hold out despite being surrounded for several hours and was only taken out by a direct hit from a modified Armoured Vehicle Royal Engineers (AVRE) tank of the 82nd Assault Squadron shooting a large Petard bomb directly into its rear entrance at 1600hrs. Defenders located in surrounding buildings had to be rooted out in fierce house to house fighting.

To the West of Le Hamel, 47 Commando came under fire from defenders at Ste Come de Fresne as they landed. Fifteen of their sixteen boats were damaged, they lost all of their signalling equipment and also took forty-

three casualties. Once off the beach, 47 Commando headed west towards the small fishing port of Port-en-Bessin, where plans were to meet up with the Americans coming off Omaha Beach. Given the tragic events already unfolding on Omaha however, and given that 47 Commando do not arrive at their objective until 2230 on D-Day, there was to be no link up that day — but they would take Port-en-Bessin on D-Day+1.

Also to the West, the 1st Hampshires and 1st Dorsets, with the help of naval support fire ,would successfully take Arromanches in the late afternoon — an important gain as it had been designated one of the future sites for a floating Mulberry Harbour.

The feared strongpoint at La Riviere had suffered more from the bombardment than Le Hamel but was still fit to fight. Its main 88mm gun had a clear view along the beach and rained down shells knocking out AVREs and flail tanks alike until it was taken out by a tank from the Westminster Dragoons which fired a 40lb Petard charge directly into its aperture. Clearing out the remaining resistance at La Riviere fell to the 5th East Yorkshires with some tank support. They achieved this with the support of flamethrower Crocodile tanks by 1000 but at the cost of over ninety men and no few tanks.

Assaulting to the east were the 6th Battalion, the Green Howards. A Company

of the Howards found themselves pinned down by a combined 105mm gun emplacement and a pillbox with a machine gun. The 105mm was quickly silenced by a supporting tank from the 4th/7th Royal Dragoon Guards but the machine gun pillbox proved more resilient until it was charged by Lance-Corporal Joyce, who climbed up on the sea wall, threw a grenade inside through the gun slit and then ordered the survivors out at gunpoint.

Elsewhere, CSM Stan Hollis and D Company moved forward to tackle a gun battery at Mont Fleury. Before they could reach it, however, they came upon a nest of pillboxes joined up by defensive trenches. CSM Hollis stormed the first pillbox, exchanging fire with its occupants as he ran forward. Somehow he reached his objective untouched, stuck his Sten gun through the gun slit and emptied it into the defenders inside. Then he scrambled onto the roof, hurled a grenade through the slit for good measured, reloaded and then accepted the surrender of the dazed German survivors. He then dropped into a trench and began to assault a second pillbox. The occupants wisely surrendered. In one single action, it's estimated that Hollis took as many as thirty prisoners — and his extraordinary actions on D-Day were far from finished.

When D Company eventually reached the Mont Fleury battery, they found it deserted. Its defenders had fled. The combined companies of the 6th Green Howards then moved on to take Crepon where they met determined resistance. The 6th decided that — rather than allowing themselves to be held up — B and C companies would skirt the village at a safe distance while D Company was instructed to do the fighting. The commander of D Company had been killed earlier in the day and CSM Hollis now found himself in charge. His men were successful in rooting the Germans out of Crepon. Leaving the village on the road to Bayeux however, he was fortunate to spot a concealed field gun supported by Mg42 Spandau machine guns in an ambush position in the hedgerow up ahead. Hollis picked up a PIAT anti-tank weapon and, supported by two Bren gunners, personally assaulted the concealed position. As Hollis blasted away with the PIAT, the accompanying Bren gunners were spotted and hit. With the artillery piece now opening fire on him, Hollis gave the order to withdraw. He made it to safety, only to discover that his two men were still trapped. Without a second's thought, Hollis flung down his PIAT, grabbed a Bren gun and started running towards his men, firing as he ran.

The two trapped Bren gunners used his covering fire to escape and all three men were soon back to safety. For his actions here — and his wild attack on the pillboxes near Mont Fleury earlier — CSM Hollis was awarded the Victoria Cross — the only man to win Britain's highest award for gallantry on D-Day.

By the end of the day, the 6th Green Howards were just one mile outside of St Leger.

To their south and east, other British forces from the 7th Green Howards (with tank support) had broken through to the village of Creully — five miles south of the beaches — by 1200. Here they seized an important bridge over the River Seulles and found only Ost troops who fell over themselves to surrender. Elements then pushed on to the important N13 road at St. Leger. Those forces remaining behind in Creully however, then got caught up in a ferocious tank action. Armour from the 4th/7th Dragoon Guards had nervously made their way through Creully and dispersed into the cornfields to the south. Here, they were suddenly hit by determined gunfire from concealed German positions manned by the Kampfgruppe Meyer and two British tanks were blown apart in just a few seconds. Another tank was lost as the Shermans sped for cover. Artillery support was called in which destroyed the German position and virtually wiped out the Kampfgruppe Meyer (certainly it did for Meyer himself), but straight afterwards the Dragoons and the men of the 7th were hit by another artillery bombardment — this time from one of their own warships. Frantically trying to call off the strike over their radios as they went, the Dragoons and the Howards retreated back towards Cruelly — only to be blitzed from the air by a USAAF P-47 Thunderbolt. The supposedly friendly aircraft made two blazing passes over his own tanks before the Dragoons could pop orange smoke to let the pilot know they were 'friendlies'. Later in the day, the British forces gathered in the east would also come under attack from small groups of Luftwaffe bombers — some of the very few German air missions flown on D-Day.

On D-Day, the British succeeded in landing 25,000 men and 2,100 vehicles on Gold Beach, for the loss of 1,100 soldiers dead, missing and wounded. Over 1,000 German prisoners were taken. Bayeux would be captured on the following day with help from the French Resistance. The 151st Brigade did succeed in cutting the road and railway from Bayeux to Caen on the first day, while elements of the 69th Brigade made contact with Canadian forces from Juno by nightfall — the only successful link up between any beaches on D-Day.

JUNO BEACH

'The bombardment having failed to kill a single German or silence one weapon, these companies had to storm their position 'cold' and did so without hesitation.'

Official War Diarist, Royal Winnipeg Rifles

Responsibility for storming Juno Beach — one of the three D-Day beaches assigned to British and Commonwealth forces — was given to the Canadians. They were expected to want revenge for Dieppe.

The area designated Juno Beach was located between Sword and Gold Beaches, stretching out for six miles from La Rivière in the west to St. Aubin in the east, and centred on the small port of Courseulles-sur-Mer — the best defended German position of all three non-American beaches. From the surf, strips of beach stretched up to dunes or a high sea wall. Houses and holiday villas were lined along its entire length in between small fishing villages and resort towns.

Responsibility for defending the area had been placed with the German 716th Infantry Division, under the command of Lieutenant-General Wilhelm Richter. They were comprised of the usual sub-standard infantry to be found along the Atlantic Wall — teenagers, old men, the partially disabled and questionably loyal Ost soldiers. Richter could only spare some 400 men to defend this area, and so chose to position virtually all of them guarding the beaches. Some were assigned to the designated strongpoints — most of which were

OPP. PAGE: Canadian infantry soldiers land on the beaches of Juno Beach

BELOW L-R: Canadian Infantrymen in a LCA going ashore from H.M.C.S. Prince Henry; Royal Canadian Navy Beach Commando "W" landing on Mike Beach, Juno sector of the Normandy beachhead; Second-wave troops of 9th Canadian Infantry Brigade, probably Highland Light Infantry of Canada, disembarking with bicycles from LCI(L)s onto '*Nan White*' Beach, Juno Area at Bernieres-sur-Mer

still in the process of construction — whilst others were hidden in abandoned houses along the seafront, protected by sandbags, layers of barbed wire and minefields and equipped with machine guns and anti-tank weapons.

Facing them were the assault troops from the 3rd Canadian Infantry Division under Major-General Rod Keller, which actually comprised about 15,000 Canadians and 9,000 British troops. They would be supported by the 2nd Armoured Brigade. Their objectives were to cut the Caen-Bayeux road, advance to the Caen-Bayeux railway line and assault and take Caen's Carpiquet Airport. British Royal Marines from 48 Commando would also take part, most notably to destroy the German strongpoint at Langrune-sur-Mer near Ste Aubin before linking up with 41 Commando ranging out from Sword Beach. Canadian troops would then link up with Gold.

The RAF and RCAF had bombed the German positions on Juno beach from 23.30 the previous night — but had missed. Due largely to bad weather and low cloud cover, not a single German position had been hit. The Canadian

assault troops had been told they could expect next to no opposition. It was not to be the case.

Over 360 vessels codenamed Force J were assembled off Juno on the early morning of 6 June, including the British cruisers Belfast and Diadem and eleven destroyers. The invasion began at 0530 with the despatch of LCTs carrying DD tanks. As they rode in, the naval bombardment erupted. Battleships, cruisers and destroyers led by HMS Belfast all unleashed massive salvos against the coastal defences. USAAF aircraft joined them, but visibility was still poor and the aircrew were so afraid of hitting their own ships that they passed right over the coastal defences and unloaded their bombs over the bocage farmland to the rear.

More and more waves of assault craft had set off after the DD tanks by now and the tanks, M7 Priest self-propelled guns and the 25lb artillery guns on board joined in with the bombardment of the beaches, as did eight rocket-carrying landing craft each sending up 1,000 rounds. With the rough seas, the firing was inevitably wild and one rocket even brought down a Spitfire swooping in to strafe the beach.

The bombardment stopped at 0730 precisely, which gave the Germans a valuable half hour in which to recover and prepare. The first Allied troops were meant to land at 0745 but were delayed almost a quarter of an hour by seas so rough and full of troughs that the landing vessels could barely keep sight of one another. The landing craft encountered virtually no fire from the German's big guns as they came in, just a smattering of machine gun fire and mortar rounds bursting in the water. They soon discovered why. General Richter had chosen to

range his most lethal artillery on the beaches themselves, rather than out to sea.

The DD tanks reached the beach first, having been released from their LCTs to swim the final 7,000 yards to shore. Behind them came specialised teams of demolition engineers to tackle the obstructions and the mines protecting them. Minutes later the first assault troops arrived in their landing craft, and a number hit mines or were torn up and sunk by underwater obstacles even before they could release their men. In all, about 30% of all landing craft at Juno Beach would be lost over the day. Those who landed safely found themselves immediately under heavy flanking fire on the run up the beach and the first wave suffered a 50% casualty rate. Bridge-carrying '*Funnies*' formed ramps to help the survivors scale the high sea wall. '*Crabs*' too scaled the wall and started clearing the minefields at the front of occupied buildings, then the troops were swiftly caught up in house-to-house fighting. Back on the beach, machine guns in pillboxes continued to mow down men until they were dealt with by the flamethrower tanks.

As expected, Courseulles proved to offer the hardest opposition. It was initially assaulted by two companies of the Regina Rifle Regiment at 0809. A Company found itself pinned down for a while, sheltering against the seawall as it was pounded by a battery of one 88mm gun supported by 75mm and 50mm artillery pieces. Fortunately, fourteen DD Sherman tanks from the 1st Hussars had also made it ashore in the area and soon began duelling with the German guns, taking the pressure off the infantry. The tanks succeeded in knocking out the 88mm and the 50mm in quick succession, but the 75mm managed to fire off almost 200 rounds before it too was destroyed. As the duel raged, A Company advanced off the sea wall and assaulted the trenches surrounding the German gun positions in

a series of brutal close quarter actions. The company suffered a total of 45 dead on D-Day, mostly due to the initial artillery shelling and the subsequent storming of the trenches. By contrast, B Company met virtually no opposition as they seized their designated area of the port. In the middle of the madness, a café just 100 yards back from the beach opened up and began serving wine.

At Bernieres, B Company of the Queen's Own Rifles also found themselves in serious difficulty when their assault boats carried them too far to the east and dropped them directly in the sights of an 88mm artillery piece supported by seven machine gun nests. Worse, the DD Tanks they were expecting to support them had not been launched because of the high seas. They were on their own, and took whatever desperate shelter they could find behind the obstacles at the water's edge. Casualties swiftly mounted — 65 dead or injured. Their position was untenable. Finally, Lieutenant W.G. Herbert, assisted by two of his men, made a mad dash right up the sands to the sea wall. Incredibly, all three of them made it and they proceeded to knock out the nearest German strongpoint with rifles, a Sten gun and grenades. Taking Bernieres was to be the costliest action on Juno Beach, with desperate bayonet charges made through barbed wire mazes to clear machine gun nests. The village was eventually taken by the Queen's Own Rifles with assistance from Quebec's Régiment de la Chaudière, who arrived in the second wave.

Once Bernieres had been taken, troops found it difficult to advance beyond the town because of fire coming from German positions in nearby Beny-sur-Mer. Heavy support artillery was directed against the village and the Queen's Own Rifles were able to take it by 1400. They then turned on German artillery batteries to the east of the village, with fire support from HMCS Algonquin off the coast.

At the eastern end of Juno, the North Shore Regiment arrived at St. Aubin at 0740 to discover that the concrete strongpoint there remained untouched by both the barrage and the bombers. Two Canadian tanks were almost immediately knocked out by the strongpoint's 50mm gun and it continued to bombard the troops as they made the 100 yard dash out of the surf and up against the sea wall. More casualties were sustained from beach mines. The Canadians replied with everything they had, including anti-tank guns, Sherman tanks and a Royal Marine Centaur armed with a 95mm howitzer. The 50mm gun managed to fire off seventy-five rounds before it was finally destroyed. Half the Germans defending the strongpoint were killed in the action and a further 48 surrendered.

48 Commando were meant to follow the North Shore Regiment in after the Canadians had control of the beach, but it was still far from secure by the

OPP. PAGE: Canadian soldiers on Juno Beach, 6 June 1944

BELOW L—R: A German prisoner captured by Canadian troops at Langrune sur Mer, 7 June 1944; Two German officers in a group of prisoners who surrendered to Canadian troops in Courseulles-sur-Mer — June 6, 1944; Corporal Victor Deblois of the Chaudière Regiment questions two German prisoners captured by Canadian troops at Juno Beach

time the Commandos came in at 0930. Some of their boats hit mines. Others overturned in the fierce swell of the surf. Fierce mortar fire took its toll. By the time the Commandos were off the beach and organising themselves for their objective, they found that they had lost all but one of their mortars, every single machine gun — and half of their men.

Fighting continued for a full two hours all along Juno Beach but by just after 1000 the Canadian forces were already landing their reserves and encountering little opposition. Almost inevitably, there was now a traffic jam on the beach, with men, tanks and vehicles awaiting their turn to go forward — and the wounded and German POWs waiting to be ferried out to the ships. They were hampered by large swathes of uncleared minefields. At St. Aubin things became so bad that incoming Brigades had to be diverted to Bernieres. It was little better there. It has been suggested that the 'traffic jam' was the only reason why the Canadians failed to achieve their D-Day objectives. Men and armour simply couldn't be freed up quickly enough.

Once the strongpoints and coastal houses had been neutralised and cleared,

the Canadians started to move inland. At 1435, orders were given for the 7th, 8th and 9th Infantry Brigades to move forward to their next objectives, with armoured support. The Germans of the 726 Regiment meanwhile were gathering in St. Croix in the hopes of mustering up a counter attack but they were spotted and broken up.

Fighting also continued against pockets of resistance in St. Aubin until 1800, but by this time the North Nova Scotia Regiment had progressed and was only three miles outside of Caen, although they were in no position to start any meaningful assault on the city.

Caen had not been taken on D-Day as Montgomery had (rather optimistically) hoped, and fighting in St. Aubin prevented the Royal Marines from linking up with Sword Beach by 2100 hours. At this time, all operations were halted for the night amid fears of a German armoured counterattack from the 21st Panzer Division. They had been blocked by determined resistance from Strongpoint WN26 at Lagrune with its 50mm guns, and two determined and bloody assaults had failed to dislodge the defenders. In fact, none of the Canadian objectives on D-Day had been met, Three Canadian tanks had actually made it as far as the Caen-Bayeux railway line but then returned behind their own lines for safety.

On the plus side, casualties on Juno were only half of that which had been anticipated — 1,000 dead or wounded rather than twice that. Most important of all, Canadian forces were now deeper into France than any other units.

SWORD BEACH

'If you don't succeed in throwing the British into the sea we shall have lost the war

General Marcks to Colonel Oppeln, 22nd Regiment, 21st Panzer Division

'Good morning commandoes and bloody good luck'

signal sent from HMS Stork to LCI carrying Lord Lovat ashore

Stretching for two miles between Lion-sur-Mer and Ouistreham, Sword was the Easternmost of the five invasion beaches and the one nearest to the city of Caen. Caen enticingly was less than ten miles away and it seemed to the Allied High Command that, if luck was with them, it could be secured fast by the 3rd Infantry Division. The troops were also required to relieve elements of the 6th Airborne who were still fighting to keep hold of strategic bridges over the River Orne and the Caen Canal.

Like the other British beaches, Sword comprised a beach followed by dunes and a coast road. The homes and businesses behind the road had been abandoned by their original owners, and some were now occupied and fortified by the Germans behind barbed wire and minefields.

OPP. PAGE: The monitor HMS ROBERTS, part of Bombarding Force 'D' off Le Havre, shelling German gun batteries in support of the landings on Sword area, 6 June 1944

BELOW L-R: The Royal Navy's big guns support the Allied armies in Normandy on board the cruiser HMS SIRIUS in the Sword area; The view from LCT 610 carrying Sherman tanks of 13th/18th Royal Hussars during the initial assault on Queen Red beach, Sword area, in front of strongpoint 'Cod', circa 0800 hrs, 6 June 1944; Commandos of 1st Special Service Brigade led by Brigadier Lord Lovat (in the water, to the right of his men) land on Queen Red beach, Sword area, c. 0840 hours, 6 June 1944

The big gun naval bombardment was followed by waves of Allied warplanes. By 0530, the first wave of LCTs carrying DD tanks had set off from the invasion force assembled off Sword, guided in by a green light and a sonar beacon from a British midget submarine positioned on the surface close offshore. X23 had been sitting on the bottom awaiting the invasion since 4 June, its five-man crew passing the time by playing cards, eating baked beans and grumbling about not being able to smoke. Following the LCTs with the DDs came the boats carrying the twenty-five 'Funnies' and the first wave of assault troops from the South Lancashire and East Yorkshire Regiments. The DDs were meant to have been launched some 7,000 yards offshore, but because the sea conditions were so bad they were released closer to 5,000 yards. The tanks struggled in the water under their own power and some sank with their crews trapped inside. One was torn apart and sunk when it was hit by the bow of its own LCT. The remaining armour 'swam' forward only with great difficulty. The DDs were meant to land first, but they made such poor headway they were

easily overtaken by the boats carrying the '*Funnies*' and the Infantry.

As the boats and swimming tanks headed in — and X23 slipped away home to England — artillery pieces on the landing craft began to bombard the shore, each with one hundred shells to expend. At 10,000 yards the 7th Field Regiment's self-propelled guns joined in from their boats too. As they drew closer to the shore, high explosive rounds were swapped for smoke shells to help hide the landing craft from the German gun emplacements. USAAF and RAF fighter planes swept overhead to strafe and bomb the beaches. The 155mm guns of Le Havre got into a duel with the guns of HMS Warspite and did not target the smaller boats. There was little fire too from the Germans on the beach area, just mortars and machine guns — but they were quickly joined by the big 88mm guns firing from strongpoints a mile or two inland.

Troops from the 2nd Battalion, East Yorkshire Regiment, were treated to a spirited recitation from Shakespeare's Henry V over their boat tannoy as they went in, read with gusto by Major C.K. '*Banger*' King while Lord '*Mad Bastard*'

Lovat of the 1st Special Service Brigade (Commando) had his personal piper, Bill Millin, play a stirring Highland Reel on one of the commando boats. When the Commandos finally hit the beach, Millin played Highland Laddie as he strutted up the sand. (Captured Germans later admitted that they hadn't shot at him because they felt sorry for him and thought he was insane). '*Good show the piper!*' said Lord Lovat approvingly at the top of the beach.

The '*Funnies*' and the Infantry hit the beach at almost exactly the same time spread across a mile of beach between the villages of Ouistreham and Lion sur Mer. As the ramps came down and the assault troops stormed the beach, Royal Marine frogmen dropped into the water and began to work on dismantling the beach obstacles. The DD Tanks finally swam in shortly after. Thirty-three of the forty tanks had survived the journey in. The tanks took less than a minute to shed their floatation skirts and struts, before pounding the line of German defenders with hard suppressive fire, trying to stop the machine gunners from cutting down the troops trying to get up the beach. Once into the dunes, it was the turn of the infantry to engage with the enemy,

as the DD tanks tried to advance off the beach to further support them. The landed '*Funnies*' were also hard at work, Crab flail tanks exploding mines and clearing paths off the beach, while others laid bridges over the sea wall. One bridge-carrier even succeeded in putting a German anti-tank gun position out of action — by dropping its bridge section directly on top of it.

Men of the East Yorks found themselves pinned down by Strongpoint 0880 — codenamed Cod — a large defensive work well over 1,000 foot long comprising a heavily reinforced pillbox supported by zig-zagging trenches. The stalemate was broken by Lieutenant Bell-Walker of B Company who single-handedly outflanked the position and managed to toss a grenade through the pillbox slit before emptying his Sten gun through the opening. He succeeded in knocking out 0880, but died almost immediately after, shot by a supporting machine gun position.

The beach assault was relatively successful and the fighting was virtually done by 0830, when the first brew-up of tea on liberated French soil began in earnest. The honour would go to the South Lancashire Regiment. The Mayor of Colleville-sur-Mer even thought it safe enough to come out in his full official regalia to welcome the British to France. The number of men the Germans had provided for the immediate defence of the coast was in the region of a mere three hundred — but as troops began to head over the road and inland they encountered more opposition. Just under a mile from the beach lay a heavy strongpoint with 75mm, 37mm and 50mm guns, supported by three 81mm mortar positions and five pits each bristling with multiple machine guns. The troops facing this were held up for three hours trying to storm it,

OPP. PAGE: British troops and naval beach parties on Sword Beach

BELOW L-R: A jumble of infantry, carriers and other vehicles on Sword Beach on the morning of 6 June; Troops of 3rd Infantry Division on Queen Red beach, Sword area, circa 0845 hrs, 6 June 1944. In the foreground are sappers of 84 Field Company Royal Engineers, part of No.5 Beach Group, identified by the white bands around their helmets. Behind them, medical orderlies of 8 Field Ambulance, RAMC, can be seen assisting wounded men; Men of a headquarters unit take shelter behind vehicles on Sword Beach

and it took the combined might of men from the East Yorks, South Lancs, 5th Battalion Kings Regiment, 4 Commando and Bren Gun carriers from the 2nd Battalion Middlesex Regiment all working together to finally crack it.

Back on the beach, engineers and '*Funnies*' worked frantically to clear German obstacles and minefields as well as wrecked Allied armour, in order to free up the exits off the beach as more and more men, vehicles and supplies came in. Also coming in was the tide, making the useable area of beach progressively smaller. The invasion force's fifty self-propelled guns were still stuck in the surf and were trying to be at least of some use, by firing at targets inland when they received calls for help. At midday, the decision was taken to suspend all further landings for half an hour to allow the jam on the beach to at least partially clear.

Part of the problem was that armour could only move off the beaches from a single exit (although there were several that could be used by infantry.) They needed to head west and then take the road to Hermanville, which was little

more than a narrow causeway over deliberately flooded marshland. Once on the road at least the immediate front was clear, as men of the South Lancs had already advanced on Hermanville and taken the village, effectively dealing with the two hundred German troops defending it.

The Commandos, who enjoyed a strong Free French contingent, had taken heavy losses on the initial beach assault. 25% of their number had been lost by the time they reached the beach wall. This however did not stop them from pressing on towards their objectives with a bracing eight mile march. They first took a coastal battery — only to find that its big guns had already been moved to relative safety inland several days earlier. They then moved on to try and join up with the British airborne troops who were still holding on to Pegasus Bridge. At 1300, the Commandos achieved their objective, linking up with the airborne soldiers. As they shook hands and exchanged pleasantries, they were plied with champagne by a local café owner while still under sniper fire. Their position was precarious — there were relatively few reinforcing commandos and the main beach force had yet to reach them — but they were now in a more secure position than they had previously enjoyed. (The glider men had fought off several German counterattacks during that night. Earlier that morning, they had been saluted by a flight of low-flying Spitfires who marked their achievement with Victory Rolls over their heads — and by dropping a bundle of morning papers).

Elsewhere, the 3rd Division's move inland was being spearheaded by 1st Battalion, the Suffolk Regiment who were the designated reserves for the 8th Infantry Brigade. At their official assembly point inland, they met up with some

Canadian paratroopers who were very much in the wrong place and not a little lost. Eager to get into the war, they became honorary members of the Suffolks. After taking Colleville, the Suffolks moved on to a strongpoint codenamed Morris. It was of standard design with inner and outer tangles of barbed wire separated by a minefield. The Suffolks expected at least six machine guns to open up on them but met no resistance. Suspecting a trap, the British troops decided to tear a hole through the outer barbed wire entanglement with Bangalore torpedoes and then call down supporting artillery fire. Before they had a chance to detonate the torpedoes however, a white flag appeared and sixty-seven Germans came out to surrender. They had had quite enough, having been both shelled by the Royal Navy and bombed by USAAF over the course of the morning. Simultaneously, the East Yorkshires took out another strongpoint — codenamed Daimler — with four 77mm guns all facing the beach. A number of prisoners were taken, including one German who — in the hope of better treatment — offered to trade his pornography collection. The victorious troops were at first prevented from enjoying a captured cache of

wines and beers found at the strongpoint, until the company sergeant major decided he rather fancied a drop himself and relented.

Strongpoint Hillman proved an altogether tougher proposition. It was 600 yards wide and boasted twelve big guns protected by nine foot thick concrete casemates. Here were 300 soldiers from the 736th Grenadier Regiment and — despite it being designated as a priority target — Hillman had not been substantially hit by either the naval bombardment or from the air.

Just after 1pm, the Suffolks managed to call in a five minute bombardment on the strongpoint, joining in with their own mortars and the guns of their supporting tanks. Following that, a breaching platoon was sent to crawl through the surrounding cornfield and deploy Bangalores against the outer field of barbed wire. This was done, and more men moved in to begin work on clearing a path through the minefield. More Bangalores were then expended against the inner wire, successfully tearing a path through it. It was not until an assault platoon attempted to storm the gap that the Germans opened up, but when they did it was to lethal effect. As the Suffolks desperately found cover in the deserted slit trenches surrounding the big gun emplacements, their platoon commander, Lieutenant Powell, blasted away at one of the machine gun positions with a PIAT anti-tank weapon. He got off three shots at it, but to no effect. The assault party were now well and truly pinned down and taking casualties fast. Tanks tried to help them, but even their 75mm HE shells had next to no effect on the concrete casemates. The tanks then tried to move up through the gap in Hillman's defences, giving cover to troops crouching behind them. The gunners from Hillman swiftly responded, knocking out two British tanks and effectively blunting the attack.

OPP. PAGE: Troops from 3rd Division, some with bicycles, move inland from Sword Beach, 6 June

BELOW L-R: The British 2nd Army: Sherman DD (Duplex Drive) tanks of 'B' Squadron, 13/18th Royal Hussars, and men of No 4 Commando advancing towards Ouistreham.; Royal Marine Commandos attached to 3rd Division for the assault on Sword Beach move through Colleville-sur-Orne on their way to relieve forces at Pegasus Bridge; The British 2nd Army: Men of No 4 Commando engaged in house to house fighting with the Germans at Riva Bella, near Ouistreham

The failure to take Hillman was having knock-on effects too. The Norfolk Regiment was unable to pass and had to skirt the area, only to be surprised by German forces in a cornfield. Forty Norfolks were killed or wounded, some by friendly fire in all the confusion.

Back at Hillman, the Suffolk's supporting tanks had actually been called away to deal with another threat, and the troops had to wait until 1615 when replacement tanks of the Staffordshire Yeomanry finally reached them. Their guns were no more effective than the previous tanks had been, but they provided good cover for the infantry as they finally got up close to the casemates. Finally, his patience having snapped, Private Titch Hunter advanced on the main position, firing his Bren gun from his hip. Others followed his example, slammed up against the concrete at a run and tipped a wealth of hand grenades down the position's ventilation shafts. Doors were also blown off using explosive charges. After that, the surviving Germans

began to surrender and by 2000 hours the fighting was over. For his actions, Private Hunter won the Distinguished Conduct Medal.

Elsewhere, to the West, serious trouble was brewing. The Germans were preparing for a determined counter-attack — the only major counter-attack to be attempted on D-Day. At 0900 that morning, General Hermann von Oppeln-Bronikowski of the 22nd Regiment of the 21st Panzer Division had been given instructions to tackle the paratrooper forces that had landed the previous night. He had tried, but as his Panzer IV armour moved it was repeatedly attacked by Allied fighters on strafing and bombing runs and had become pinned down on several occasions. By mid-day, his orders had changed. Now he was to go back through Caen (which was under constant bombing attack), meet up with the elite 192nd Panzergrenadier Regiment and then launch a joint counter-attack starting at 1900, slicing between the Allied forces on Sword and Juno Beach, '*If you don't succeed in throwing the British into the sea we shall have lost the war,*' his superior General Marcks told him starkly. He now had ninety-eight tanks to change the course of the war.

The 192nd Panzergrenadiers successfully broke through to the sea at 2000 hours on D-Day. Manoeuvring in between the British forces from Sword and

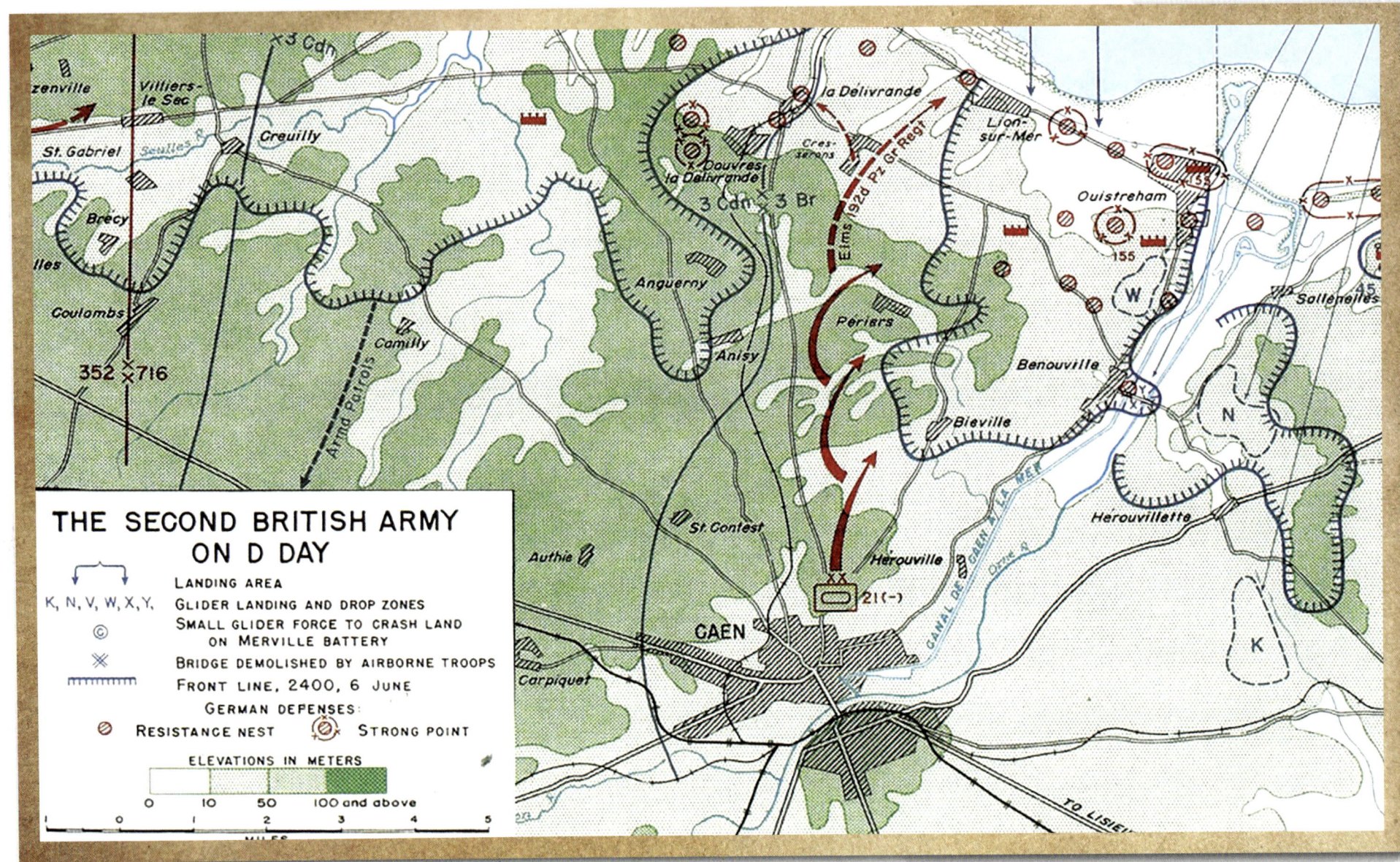

THE SECOND BRITISH ARMY ON D DAY

- ⤵ LANDING AREA
- K, N, V, W, X, Y, GLIDER LANDING AND DROP ZONES
- ⓒ SMALL GLIDER FORCE TO CRASH LAND ON MERVILLE BATTERY
- ✼ BRIDGE DEMOLISHED BY AIRBORNE TROOPS
- ⬚⬚⬚ FRONT LINE, 2400, 6 JUNE
- GERMAN DEFENSES:
- ⊘ RESISTANCE NEST   ⊘ STRONG POINT

ELEVATIONS IN METERS

0 10 50 100 and above

0   1   2   3   4   5
MILES

RIGHT: General Hermann von Oppeln-Bronikowski

OPP. PAGE: An operational map showing The Second British Army, the "J" Day. Down below, in the center, the city of Caen. Top right, Sword Beach. Between the two, at Bénouville and crossing the Orne river and the Caen Canal to the sea, the Bénouville and Ranville bridges, later renamed "Pegasus Bridge" and "Horsa Bridge". The red arrows indicate German counteroffensive attempts

the Canadians on Juno, they met next to no opposition — but their arrival did alert the Allies that something major was about to take place and, by the time the 22nd Regiment moved to join their infantry (having already lost six more tanks to ground attacks by rocket-firing RAF Typhoons), both Canadians and British were ready and waiting with serious armour and artillery including three troops of seventeen pounder Sherman Fireflys. Oppeln-Bronikowski lost five panzers to Allied fire from the advancing Shropshires within the first couple of minutes of the engagement, and then fighter-bombers from the RCAF swept in to rip apart further German armour. A further six panzers fell to the British guns on Périers Ridge. The German tank strike ground to an abrupt halt as the 22nd desperately dug in, leaving the Panzergrenadiers to fend for themselves. The German infantry suffered hard losses from Allied air attacks and had little in the way of anti-aircraft guns to defend themselves. When they spotted Allied airborne glider reinforcements coming in later that night, they began to retreat again, fearing being cut off and surrounded.

The need to tackle the immediate threat of the German counterattack had put paid to any hope of taking Caen on D-Day. Troops were ordered to dig in where they were. Troops of the King's Shropshire Light Infantry had made it some distance down the Hermanville to Caen road, reaching Biéville-Beuville, with the help of some self-propelled guns, but they too had been forced to stop short because of the threat of counterattack.

29,000 men and 2,603 vehicles were put ashore on D-Day at Sword Beach. The price was 630 killed, wounded or missing. British and Canadian forces would link up on D-Day +1.

D-DAY PLUS...

In 1943 Eisenhower made a £5 bet with Montgomery that the war would be over by Christmas 1944. He lost the bet.

Coming to the realisation that Normandy Landings were '*the real thing*' and no mere diversion, Hitler had personally ordered that there was to be no withdrawal of any German forces. They would stand and fight. British and Canadian forces fought for weeks to try and secure Caen where the bulk of German resistance was initially located. Even when they succeeded in advancing beyond Caen late July, the Allied forces in the area still made only slow progress.

Meanwhile, the Americans broke out of the Cotentin Peninsula at Avranches on 31 July, sending German forces tumbling back in disarray. Twenty One German Divisions were trapped at Falaise in August — and almost entirely obliterated by the ruthless application of Allied Air Power. The survivors retreated towards the Seine, despite the Fuhrer's orders.

On 25 August 1944, Allied troops entered Paris. By 3 September, Britain's Guards Armoured Division was in Brussels. The same day, the 11th Armoured Division captured the massive port facility at Antwerp. Allied forces here were less than one hundred miles from the Rhine and Germany. Ahead of them was a one hundred mile gap in the German defences. In the air, the Allied air forces could count on over 14,000 warplanes. The Luftwaffe could barely scrounge up 570. German armour was so depleted that they now had just one hundred tanks west of the Rhine. The

Allies had over 2,000. Tragically, however, the Allies did not know this. After a daring — and overambitious — attempt to seize a bridge over the Rhine at Arnhem ended in failure, the Allied attack started to stall. The Germans took advantage, hastily reinforcing in their most vulnerable area. Such an opportunity would never again present itself and the Allies paid in blood. Two thirds of all casualties suffered by Allied troops in the liberation of Europe happened after September 1944.

In December 1944, Hitler threw almost everything into a last ditch counter attack in the Ardennes. In what became known as the Battle of the Bulge, a massive surprise attack spearheaded by armour slammed westward into the American 1st Army in Belgium. It failed, due to determined American resistance, harsh winter conditions, a shortage of fuel and a break in the weather that let the Allied warplanes finally unleash hell on the panzers. Germany had gambled — and lost — its finest reserves.

The Allies continued to bide their time over the winter, seizing bridges over the Rhine and finally spilling out onto German soil in March 1945. From then on, their advance was slowed more by the damage to German roads done by Allied bomber fleets than by surviving German military units. By 11 April, Allied forces were on the Elbe, just sixty miles from Berlin, where they sat while Soviet forces took the German capital. On the night of 30 April, Hitler committed suicide on his Berlin bunker.

On 4 May, German forces in North West Europe officially surrendered on Luneberg Heath, the site of Montgomery's HQ. A further surrender, including all German forces was signed at Eisenhower's HQ in Reims on 7 May 1945.

'There's a graveyard in northern France where all the dead boys from D-Day are buried. The white crosses reach from one horizon to the other. I remember looking it over and thinking it was a forest of graves. But the rows were like this, dizzying, diagonal, perfectly straight, so after all it wasn't a forest but an orchard of graves. Nothing to do with nature, unless you count human nature.'

Barbara Kingsolver